D1127805

THE OTHER SIDE OF AUTISM

**A JOURNEY OF A MOTHER
AND DAUGHTER**

NATALIE A. KULIG
VICTORIA A. KULIG

Order this book online at www.trafford.com
or email orders@trafford.com

Most Trafford titles are also available at major online book retailers.

Print information available on the last page.

ISBN: 978-1-4907-7909-6 (sc)
ISBN: 978-1-4907-7908-9 (e)

Trafford rev. 12/08/2016

 www.trafford.com
North America & international
toll-free: 1 888 232 4444 (USA & Canada)
fax: 812 355 4082

FOREWORD

Another Side of Autism- Reflections by the Brother

By Zachary Kulig

"She looks like a strawberry!" I exclaimed, looking down at my new little sister. As I sat there staring at her with a big smile, my 7-year-old mind raced with images of all the adventures we were going to go on, all of the hours we would play together, and the stories we would share. Becoming a big brother was the proudest moment of my young life. I was unaware the journey we were about to embark on as a family would be different than the one I imagined and the responsibility I was about to be handed, I could not have anticipated.

Fast forward a few months after her birth. I remember many early mornings asking my mom, "Does she ever stop crying, mommy?" as I rubbed the sleep from my eyes. Knowing this was our normal start to the early years, I would take it upon myself to make sure I got dressed and took care of my immediate needs so my Mom and Dad could devote their time to my sister. That meant at the age of 7, waking up on my own for school, getting something to eat, and making sure I had all my things in order so we could leave right on schedule. Not being another burden to my parents was the best thing I could do to not add to any complications that might have come up that day.

I am thankful for learning a lesson in self-reliance so young, because it showed me how important being a support role and a team player were in everyday life. It meant keeping the balance of autism in check, even if it meant leaving restaurants and loud arcades early, not going to amusement parks or carnivals as a young kid (but boy did that change once Vicky realized how much fun roller coasters were), and many other busy activities. These are lessons that I have to thank my little sister for.

Vicky, thank you for teaching me how to grow up strong and how to be compassionate towards other people and their needs. I continue to be amazed as I watch you grow up and become so independent, and I hope that my actions were a good example for you to follow. And Mom, thank you for always finding that balance in our lives, even if you did not see that you were doing just that. Thanks for always having my back and helping my sister be the best version of herself.

Many people do not understand the impact that autism has on the lives of all people who live with it. Our family story is one that shares the different moments and events that shaped our lives and gave us hope.

PART I

AUTISM

From Mom's Side

By Natalie A. Kulig

PREFACE

At age three my daughter was diagnosed with Pervasive Development Disorder, Not Otherwise Specified – a condition related to the autism spectrum disorder. It was the year 2000, and there was not nearly the assortment of resources and support groups as there is today. I found books that were so depressing I thought I would cry forever. I read books that taught me how to understand terms such as *Social Stories*, *ABA*, *Floor time*, and the *Picture Exchange System (PECS)*. I read books by Karen Black and Temple Grandin, two women with high functioning autism who told their stories in detail. Both of them made me realize I was in for a life of rollercoaster emotions: from scared to funny; from sad and confused to happy and proud. What I was not sure about was if I would ever find time to enjoy my child between all the worry and therapy sessions. I had imagined dance lessons, playing dress-up, doing hair and makeup as well as teaching her to ride a bike, study science, and get her hands dirty in the garden. Routines set in concrete were now the order of the day. I learned about sensory issues I did not even know existed, and tantrums that came out of the blue and could rarely be stopped quickly.

I thought I would be chauffeuring her to practices and recitals, not speech and occupational therapy. Before the autism diagnosis, I tried so hard to make her happy and could not figure out what I was doing wrong. The autism diagnosis changed my view of myself – did I do something that caused this? Was there any truth to the "refrigerator mom" I had come across in my early research? I had no idea how I was going to cope with this diagnosis. What made it even more challenging, was I had moved away from my family in Illinois when my husband accepted a job offer in Kentucky. "Home" was now six hours away, and my entire network of friends, family, and support was absent. I spent many hours alone, while my son was at school and my husband was at work, watching this beautiful, complicated little girl and realized that I had not a clue how to raise her. The idea of autism made me freeze into a statue of a mother who did not know which way to move. I remember coming across an article called "Don't Mourn for Us," written by Jim Sinclair (http://www.autreat.com/dont_mourn.html). The article asked us not to hate autism because autism is what makes them the person they are. The article alluded to the fact that if we hate autism then we must hate who they are. "Be sad about that, if you want to be sad about something. Better than being sad about it, though, get mad about it--and then *do* something about it" (Sinclair, 1993).

It was at that moment I realized that I did not want to look at my daughter and only see autism. I wanted to celebrate the person she was and the person she was to become. This was not easy in the first years of diagnosis. I was so consumed with reading, researching, trying different biomedical and alternative treatments, I was not enjoying our day to day life together. I felt I could only concentrate on the methods needed to shape her into what I thought she should be.

When I look back at some of the things I have been through, sometimes I laugh —because otherwise, I might cry — I rejoice in her antics and the way she perceives the world. I allow myself to laugh – at myself for some of the ridiculous things I did to make her "normal" and to laugh with her as I watched her take in the world and try and process it. So, what follows is MY story. But even greater than my funny and serious anecdotes that I share with the reader while telling my story, is the fact that my daughter has co-authored this book with me. Many people do not get to hear stories from the autism side, because many people with autism cannot verbalize their feelings. I have asked my daughter to include her story. I have asked her to share what it is like to live with autism and to add her perceptions to some of the same events I included in my stories of life with autism.

So now I lead you into one of the most personal journeys of my daughter's and my life. Autism has two sides, so I hope you laugh, cry, rejoice, and never look back…I believe the best is yet to come!

CHAPTER 1

AUTISM: THE YOUNGER YEARS

When my daughter was diagnosed with autism at the age of three, I was devastated…and relieved. For the first three years of her life, I thought that I had to be the worst parent in the world. My first child, a boy, hit all of his milestones on time, slept five hours straight at eight weeks old, and rarely had a tantrum. So how could I have given birth to this sweet little girl who never slept, had colic, and had only moments of smiles and gurgles? After my son was born, I used to watch parents struggle with children screaming in the malls, kicking in the grocery cart, and flailing in their strollers. "Ugh," I thought to myself, "Why can't those parents control their kids?" Now, I was the parent of one of those kids…and it was not fun to be on this side of the fence.

So, when her diagnosis of PDD-NOS (Pervasive Development Disorder – Not Otherwise Specified) came into play, there was a part of me that was silently relieved. I guess I was not such a bad parent after all. But after that initial "yeah, it's not my fault" feeling; tears streamed down my face. Autism. My baby girl had autism. How was I supposed to feel? What was I supposed to do? There was almost seven years between my children and I had three miscarriages between them – she was such a long awaited baby. How could my little girl have autism?

The Child Evaluation Center in Louisville, Kentucky, did her initial evaluation. Victoria's team of evaluators included a medical doctor, a psychologist, a social worker, an occupational therapist, and a physical therapist. After four hours of interviews and evaluations in a 17-page single-spaced typed report they gave their diagnosis – "It is our impression Victoria presents with a Pervasive Developmental Disorder, manifesting as communication impairments with social communication deficits, diminished imaginative play skills with some repetitive behaviors and desire to be consistent with the diagnosis of the autistic disorder."

In a nutshell, they considered her high functioning – but what exactly did that mean? The team presented articles, reference materials, suggestions on how to educate her and a sea of other information. What could they really tell us about her future? Absolutely nothing. Did she have a mental impairment? Maybe, maybe not. Would she be mainstreamed in her education? We were told to put her in a special preschool for at-risk children and see how she did in the school setting. They suggested social stories, social training, intensive behavioral intervention, and the Picture Exchange Communication System (PECS). We were to model and encourage participation in play, facilitate responsiveness to language, and provide occupational therapy. Okay, anyone speak Greek? I had absolutely no idea what any of this meant. I was a marketing manager, retired just three years earlier, to be a stay at home mom. Now they were throwing things at me, and I had absolutely no idea what they were talking about.

I felt as if we were stepping out onto a LIFE® game board. Would we spin the wheel and have a successful move or end up losing a turn? Read on – the journey is far from over.

CHAPTER 2

BEFORE DIAGNOSIS

Colic Anyone???

Ahh…the sweet smell of baby powder and the sound of rattles, and did I mention the screaming? Eight months of colic – "Does she ever stop crying," my husband would ask each night when he walked in the door after work. Really, he should have considered himself lucky; he didn't get the first four hours of the day – thank God my son was in school – only myself and the neighborhood had to endure the morning screaming fits which stopped as abruptly as they started.

Hold her? Cuddle Her? Rock Her? Adore Her? Not a chance on this planet – I was considering a move to Mars – maybe no one would hear her scream.

Emergency Room Visit!

After one or two bouts per night of screaming, I had finally had it. Something was wrong with my baby, and somebody was going to tell me why she never slept and why she was so miserable all the time. So at the ripe hour of 2 AM, I woke my husband and son and insisted we drive to the nearest emergency room. I sat in the back seat of the van trying to console this screaming child. Her face was red; her veins were bulging and she was gasping for air. We pulled into the emergency room parking lot and I gathered her writhing body in her car seat. She was crying so hard, I thought she would vomit or at least burst a vein in her bright red face.

We walked into the bright lights of the emergency room. I lead my then seven-year-old son to the seating area as my husband registered us at the desk. As I set down her car seat on the floor I was amazed – she was staring up at the fluorescent lights in the ceiling and the crying had stopped. Not only had it stopped – she was cooing and smiling – fully alert, no busted veins. It was a miracle. What was I supposed to tell the emergency room doctor now!? Maybe the doctor would think that I was the one with the problem, near a nervous breakdown from all the crying and lack of sleep! But how could I prove it now? This beautiful baby was smiling and bright-eyed. I got up and walked out of the emergency room, tears streaming down my face. My husband and son were trailing behind me. An emergency room staff member was running after us and calling out that we had already registered and would now have to sign a release to leave. All I could do is laugh.

Formula or Champagne?

A visit to my pediatrician suggested that it might be her formula causing the colic, and so began the formula roulette. After attempting every formula on the market, we finally settled on *Alimentum®* – some pre-digested formula (who predigested it, I really can't say I wanted to know) at $8 or $9 a can back in 1997. There went the budget, but at least the screaming stopped!

Nursery or Torture Chamber

Many parents plan for the birth of their new baby by creating the perfect nursery. For us it was no different. We brought up the crib our son had slept so comfortably in. We painted the room a beautiful yellow and decorated it with *Winnie the Pooh, Tigger, Piglet,* and *Eeyore*. We purchased the new toys with black and white checks with red trim – the ones that were supposed to stimulate visual learning. It was perfect! And from the day she was born, I do not recall her ever having a good night's sleep in that room. She spent most of her early months sleeping in the living room in her beautiful handmade cradle (by her dad's hands) in white linen bedding with pink and blue trim.

With the event of diagnosis of autism three years later, we found out two very fascinating things about her. First, we discovered yellow was a very agitating color for her to be around. As a matter of fact, until she was five she would not hold a yellow crayon, sit on the yellow triangle in circle time at preschool, and even though art was her favorite subject, if it meant wearing the yellow smock, she would rather not paint. Imagine that – she hated yellow so much that it interfered her ability to function. And I wondered why she wouldn't sleep in that adorable yellow nursery.

Second, we found out was she was very sensitive to patterns and colors. She used to scream and fidget when we ate at a restaurant that had red and white checkered tablecloths. And that fine eating establishment known as *Steak and Shake*, she couldn't enter one without screaming. Figured it out yet? Black and white checked patterns were as disturbing as yellow – remember those new toys and blocks for infants that stimulate visual learning? Yes, you guessed it, we didn't create a nursery, we created a torture chamber.

The Mall Police

One thing I learned the most about after her diagnosis was the effects of sensory overload. Before diagnosis, I had never heard of such a thing. As a stay-at-home mom, during the cold Chicago winters, one way to break up the day was to cruise the mall. A little window shopping, a cup of coffee and the day went by a little faster...unless of course you had a child with sensory issues!

On one such trip to a local mall with a friend, my daughter, (now a feisty two-year-old – pre-diagnosis) was flailing about in her stroller as usual. Screaming, kicking, yelling up a storm - I finally decided if I just let her free for a little while, she would be happier. So, I took her out of her stroller to let her toddle about. What I got instead was a temper tantrum right in the middle of the mall. With my friend looking on, I decided that I was not going to let the "terrible twos" get the best of me. I was going to stand firm. As she kicked and screamed and cried, I yelled to her I was leaving – she'd better get up and stop all the commotion. I hid behind a mall advertising board to see if she would get up and come and find me. Suddenly, the mall security guard was standing over her. She only cried louder with this stranger so close. He looked around the area, completely distressed, thinking that some mother just left her child in this state. I quickly came out from behind the sign trying to explain that I was just trying to teach my out of control child a lesson. He looked at me very disapprovingly. I quickly swept up my crying child and left the mall. The mental hospital was looking better and better every day.

Coming OR Going?

The next year flew by and I can honestly say that I do not have much memory of it. I continued to help at my son's school and I remember that no one offered to babysit very much (too much crying - not enough flexibility). I had a few friends who would take her for a while so I could decompress during a short walk or so my husband and I could go to the movies. The turning point came into our lives when my husband was offered a job that meant relocation to Louisville, Kentucky. It was before diagnoses and we had never left the Chicago area. We were excited for our new adventure and had no idea what a ride it would be!

CHAPTER 3

THE BIG MOVE

So our new chapter in life began – I was ready for a new adventure. It was exciting and looking for a new house was fun. The area of Kentucky we were moving to was so pretty and my husband and I felt like newlyweds again. The bonus? Housing in Kentucky was less expensive than in Illinois and we were going to move into my dream home. It was a corporate move, so we had a moving company pack our things. All I had to do was organize, sort, and get rid of stuff we didn't need to take. The moving crew packed up our life in a moving truck and off to Louisville we went. Since my daughter loved riding in cars, there were never issues with travelling...probably the only time she didn't cry!

The New Doctor

A change of address brings lots of new things. Setting up utilities, changing the phones, signing the kids up for school, and of course finding a new pediatrician. As fate would have it, my sister sent me flowers. The beautiful flowers were delivered by someone who used to live not too far from our old town back in Illinois. We talked at my doorstep and she recommended a team of pediatricians that she had taken her children to. So, I called to schedule a school physical for my son. There were four doctors in the practice, and as luck would have it – my son was seen by a pediatrician who had several autistic patients. When she met my daughter at the age of 2½, she immediately gave me her observations. "Mom, I see some delays in your child, I would like to schedule an appointment to discuss." I queried, "What kind of delays?" She said she noted some language delay and some of her movements seemed repetitive. She asked me a few questions. I felt defensive. I explained that while I felt she was hitting milestones a little later than her brother, she was fine. Besides, her brother was always ahead of the charts and she was just a little behind. I admitted that I thought she might be a little out of sync, but we did just move. We were up to our heads in boxes and my husband traveled a lot. I kept giving her excuses, wondering as I did whether I was trying to convince her or myself. As we left, she uttered some letters to me – PDD-NOS – and said, "Please bring her back, we need to evaluate her."

When we got home, I placed Vicky in front of her video – the one she watched over and over again. The coffee table held her wooden blocks, which she lined up in a row, knocked off the table, and then lined up again. "She's just a little quirky," I thought to myself. "Nothing is wrong with her. So she doesn't really talk yet, no big deal. It will come, she **is** only 2 ½ years old."

Later in the week, I did an Internet search on, what was it called - PDD-NOS? When the search came up, it pointed me to websites concerning Autism. "No way," I thought and logged off, not wishing to read anymore.

Another Trip to the Pediatrician – Still in Denial

A few months later, my son came down with strep throat, so it was another trip to the pediatrician and yes of course, the same doctor who uttered those letters, PDD-NOS. After confirming my son's strep throat, the doctor smiled at me as she watched my daughter making faces in the mirror. She was twisting her hair and making indiscriminate sounds. Now just one-month shy of her third birthday, we watched as she tuned out the world and enjoyed the place she was in, wherever that was. Okay, Okay, I knew what the doctor was looking at, and I helplessly gave into the denial. "What do we do?" I asked, feeling helpless.

The doctor referred her to the early intervention program in Kentucky. A woman came to our home to take down information. She handed me a book on Autism when she walked in. She filled out her questionnaire as my daughter stood in the dining room opening and closing the door – another one of her fascinations. Since she was almost three, she was immediately placed to into the school system – after an evaluation by the school, she was placed in pre-school with other high-risk children, ranging from mild disabilities such as hers, or maybe just lower socioeconomic situations at home. It was a diverse group of kids and I was scared to death.

She started preschool at three years old. She was not potty-trained, didn't really talk, and I was not sure how she would do at all. But thanks to a patient and incredible group of teachers and aides, we muddled along each day, hoping and praying the help she was getting would make a difference.

No More Diapers

She was still in *Pull-Ups*® at four-years-old and finally the teachers at school told me that she really need to start potty-training. I had tried and tried, but there was so much to deal with that I thought potty-training was just too hard. But her teacher had a different idea. I had to send her to school in real underwear with a change of clothes. I thought the teachers were nuts. Why would they want to deal with real underwear instead of diapers?

My daughter would cry and fight me about having real underwear on, but she would wear them. She only had a few accidents and potty-training was successful, at least at school. At home, however, the minute she walked through the door, she would strip off her clothes and search for her *Pull-Ups*®. It was as if this diaper was her security blanket. Then came the fateful day when we used the last one. As we threw it in the trash, we waved "bye-bye" to the last *Pull-Up*®. She was finally potty-trained.

Locked in the Basement

The home we owned in Kentucky was beautiful and spacious. It was a brick home with over 3000 square feet in the main living space and 800 finished in the basement. We spent many afternoons in our basement playing in the "centers" I had created to teach her how to play, based on Dr. Greenspan's Floor Play method (*Your Special Needs Child*). The basement door had a deadbolt lock on it – from the upstairs. I really never took that much notice of it as we did not lock it – ever! But one day, my daughter ran upstairs and decided to turn the deadbolt – with me still in the basement. When I tried to get upstairs, I realized the door was locked. I knocked on the door and could hear her on the other side, calling my name. "Honey," I cried, "Honey, open the door for Mommy, turn the lock, okay?" She still did not talk much at this point and could not follow a string of directions. She became panicked when I did not come through the door and I became panicked because I could not open the door. There was no key and I was afraid to break down the door because she was on the other side. Thank goodness there was a phone in the basement. But who do I call? My husband was out of town (again) and my son was at school. As we had just moved to Kentucky, I really didn't know all our neighbors. Our subdivision had put together a neighborhood guide and we were given one when we moved in. I tried calling the neighbors to either side of me, to no avail – no one was home. I thought about calling the police, but was very embarrassed that my four-year-old had locked me in the basement. Finally, I looked in the directory of our subdivision and found a name that looked familiar – I thought I had met them at a neighborhood gathering. When I called the house, a woman answered. It was not the neighbor I thought I had met, but it was a voice on the other end just the same. I explained my situation and asked the woman to come and let me out. She would have to punch in the garage door code and come in through the service door. I explained she would be met by a friendly golden retriever and a terrified 4-year-old. I hung up and soothingly talked to my daughter to let her know I was okay. I heard the garage door open. The woman came and opened the door. I was eternally grateful, introduced myself, explained about my daughter's autism, asked her to stay for coffee – she looked at me like I was nuts, left my house, and she never spoke to me again. I left a small gift in her mailbox to thank her for saving me, but whenever I saw her pull into her driveway, I got a quick glance, as if to say, "Oh yeah, there's the crazy woman who let her 4-year-old lock her in her basement." Oh, well!

Another Locked Door!

As I began to make new friends in my neighborhood in Kentucky, it was forever challenging to introduce Vicky to new surroundings. One of my son's friend's mom invited us over for a visit. Her youngest daughter was close to my daughter's age and her older daughter and my son were in class together. She was a breath of fresh air for me and I was so excited to engage in some adult conversation, when all of a sudden, we heard a knock on the door. My daughter had locked herself in the bathroom. But the house was older and there were no keys for these doors. There was a glass block window so we couldn't even try and open a window for an escape route. After about 45 minutes, we were finally able to pick the lock. So much for a quiet visit with new friends, at least we were invited back!

The Red Shoe Incident

One of my daughter's biggest sensory issues was clothes, although at the beginning of this journey, I didn't realize what an issue it was. Her basic wardrobe at this point was black stretch pants and a purple T-Shirt. Her shoes were Velcro gym shoes – and it was the only outfit she would wear. Well, I was sick and tired of the same old purple shirt and gym shoes. I was shopping at *Gymboree* and saw the cutest pair of little red Mary Jane shoes. I bought them and came home to put them on her. When I placed them on her feet, she ran outside screaming. As she ran around the back yard, she kicked the shoes off. I ran after her and kept putting the shoes back on – "Look how pretty, aren't they cute," I would coax. But she would have none of it. After about 15 minutes of running around the yard, repeatedly putting these shoes on and watching her take them off in a tantrum, I finally gave up. The shoes went to Goodwill. I sure hope the lady who let me out of my locked basement was not watching me that day!

Learning My Lesson – Again.

Okay, so now as you read this you're going to ask me how many times does it take for me to learn my lesson? Well, too many, I suppose. I wanted to live in a NORMAL world and my daughter would be NORMAL if it killed me. I was on my way to dying.

A dear friend of ours was getting married for the second time. We were friends since childhood, and we watched his first wife lose her battle to cancer right before our move to Kentucky. When we were invited to this particularly wonderful occasion, there was no way we were going to miss it. The kids were included on the invitation. It was an outdoor wedding in Indiana on a beautiful fall day. I purchased three different outfits for my daughter, hoping that she would wear one of them to the church and reception.

We checked into our hotel and began to dress for the church. After we were all ready, I showed my daughter the adorable outfits I bought for her. "No, No!" she cried "Purple shirt, Purple Shirt!" She wanted to wear her black pants and purple shirt – the one that she had been wearing for two days straight! I put my foot down and as we struggled and she sobbed. I put on each outfit trying to tell her how beautiful she looked and all she could do was scream and cry. The hysteria in the hotel room was too much and once again I had pushed the limits. She fell asleep in her underwear and I missed the ceremony at the church. My husband and son came back to pick us up to go to the reception. I was in my beautiful dress, my husband and son in their suits, and she was in her black leggings and purple shirt...oh well, at least we had a wonderful time at the reception.

A Birthday Party

Again, taking my cues from the NORMAL world, when her fourth birthday arrived, we decided to have a bunch of her friends over for a party. We set up games and had birthday cake and birthday hats. When the kids started to sing happy birthday, she went into a tantrum and ran upstairs to her room, slamming the door. I finally coaxed her to open the door. She opened her gifts, but the kids had to watch her from the doorway of her room. When was I going to learn?

The "Benjamin Vest"

As I said earlier, clothes were always difficult, and when she found something she loved, that was it – she owned it! So, when we were shopping for Christmas gifts, I found this adorable outfit for my nephew, who is two years younger than my daughter. When we got home, Vicky went right to the bag, pulled out this cute little faux-down sleeveless vest – that was at least two sizes too small for her – and zipped it up. She was so happy! I told her that it was a gift for her cousin, it was "Benjamin's vest." She agreed and echoed "Benjamin Vest" and wore it to school, and to bed, and to play outside, and on hot days, and cold days, and…well you get the picture. I went shopping for another present.

CHAPTER 4

AUTISM AND DEPRESSION

We have all heard the word and seen the commercials for various prescriptions to alleviate the problem. I have heard the stigma of people saying that you should just buck up and be strong. In fact, a few people have actually said that to me!

In my darkest hours, I often wondered what it would be like not to have to face another day. What would it be like not to have to wash the purple shirt again? What if the placemat on the table did not have to be perfectly perpendicular to the chair in front of it – what if I used the green dish instead of the blue dish? What if I didn't have to watch the *Jungle Book* for the 500th time that week? What would life be like if I could actually go to the mall with my child not screaming? What if my life was normal????

A visit to my physician and medication helped me begin to face my new life head on. (**Note:** It was not just medication – a good therapist to help me sort out how to deal with behavior issues was also a part of my journey back to sanity).

Importance of Connecting to a Group

Of course, Autism brings to us to a life which we did not choose. It brings to mind the story of ending up in Holland instead of going to Italy. The story was written by Emily Perl Kingsley in 1987 and titled, *Welcome to Holland*. It explores the idea that having a child with a disability is like planning a trip to one place and ending up in another.

I believe it profoundly affected me because I wanted the life parenting a child without autism, but I that is not what I got. Instead, I had to learn to navigate around all the new sights and sounds of a life with autism and learned along the way that "Holland" was as nice a place as "Italy".

I remember my first support group meeting. I had found a group that was from Southern Indiana and Northwest Kentucky. We were allowed to bring our children and it felt like a family outing. When we arrived, we realized our daughter was one of a few very young children participating in the meeting. While the children played in the gym of the building we were in, I listened to a speaker talk about I.E.P.s, 504Cs, transition programs, work programs, and group homes. I was terrified. She was only four years old! I had never given teen years and adulthood any thought yet. I went home more depressed than ever.

Finding people in similar shoes helps to make the road you walk less lonely, more bearable. I found a support group at a chiropractic children's center in Kentucky. Known as the Kentuckiana Children's Center (KCC), this group of doctors and social workers helped put together the pieces of the puzzle known as autism. I met other parents who were struggling with similar issues and children in the same age group. Some parents had so much more to deal with than myself that I began to appreciate the high functioning aspect of autism in our lives. I began to involve myself with this parent group and my daughter continued to see a very special Doctor of Chiropractic, who showed me ways of dealing with autism in a non-traditional way.

CHAPTER 5

THE END OF WHEAT AND DAIRY

I remember the day the doctor at the chiropractic center suggested I place my daughter on a gluten free/casein free diet. I remember my shock – no wheat or dairy – was she crazy? But as always, I began my research. I read a book written by Karyn Serousi, *Unraveling the Mystery of Autism and Pervasive Development Disorder*, on the benefits of the diet and why it may work. We tested my daughter's hair for toxic elements and found out that her body was holding great quantities of aluminum, mercury, arsenic, and other heavy metals. When I decided to pursue these avenues, I did so with much trepidation. I believed that they were somewhat "hocus pocus" but thought that anything was worth a try.

In my daughter's case, the diet worked wonders. After four weeks on a gluten free diet, she began speaking in 2-3 word sentences. Although her pronouns were still mixed up, "I pick you up?", she began expressing herself more and more. Her language began mirroring the tapes she was watching and although echolalia (repeating what was just said) was still very prevalent, she was trying.

I knew there were no double blind placebo tests done with 500 people in a clinical study over 5 years, but after watching my daughter, I truly believe the gluten free/casein free diet should not be overlooked by anyone. Although it is no cure for autism and not all people with autism respond to the diet as well as my daughter, the research behind the diet is viable and should be looked at closely. There is scientific research that shows how certain foods can make us feel and react. So why not look more closely at the research about the diet.

The diet is difficult in the beginning, but no more so than having a child with a peanut allergy or a diabetic child who must watch their sugar intake. Fifteen years ago when we started this diet, you could only find products in a specialty health food store, now gluten-free is everywhere. Gluten-free items are being sold at local grocery stores and you can even order gluten free items off the menu at many of your favorite restaurants. What seemed so daunting in the year 2000 now, is relatively easy in the year 2016.

We also added additional supplements to her diet. We visited a DAN (Defeat Autism Now) doctor and did yearly (or almost yearly) testing to determine what levels of the supplements she needed when she was younger. I do not recommend trying out these supplements without the direction of a doctor and the special tests that support them. For more information, locate a doctor in your area who specializes in this type of treatment.

CHAPTER 6

BREAKING THE LANGUAGE CODE

Anyone with a child on the spectrum experiences the language delay that comes with diagnosis. Echolalia seems to be the mode of conversation. Maybe they do not respond at all because they do not understand what you want. Maybe they only talk about one particular subject. This makes trying to find out what the child needs stressful for the parent and frustrating for the child.

One particular incident I remember was when my daughter was first learning a few phrases to communicate. Up until the start of the diet, most of my daughter's language was just echolalia. It was hard to communicate with someone who only repeated what was said to her. About six weeks after the diet, she began talking in complete phrases – although many of them were direct snippets from movies she had watched, she was using them appropriately. For example, her brother could easily disrupt her personal space. All he wanted to do was play with her, but she wanted nothing to do with him. Usually, this incited a tantrum to get my attention to make him leave the room. After about the 501st viewing of Disney's *The Jungle Book*, one day, she matter-of-factly looked at him and stated, "Go away and leave me alone!" At first, I thought that she actually put this string, of words together, but after the 502nd viewing of *The Jungle Book*, I realized that this is what Mowgli said to Baloo Bear. Even though the phrase was a direct quote from the movie, she used it appropriately and this was progress, in my mind anyway.

As she grew, we had to work hard on idioms, facial expressions, body language, and other nonverbal means of communication. As she progressed in school, she had to learn literary terms and how to analyze poetry and symbolism. To a concrete mind, these skills are difficult. However, with the right team of teachers, specialists, and parents always ready to explain and work with these concepts, each year became easier.

There are different schools of thought on whether or not you should let a child with autism continue to lose themselves in movies, computers, music, etc. When she began to pick up her language from movies, I took it as a positive move towards language. There were times, however, it was easy to lose her completely in her videos, so we began to limit the time she watched TV and tried to engage her in copycat playing from scenes in the movie.

"I Want Breakfast"

Another breakthrough came one morning at breakfast. She sat down at the table and looked me square in the eyes – "Mommy, I want breakfast!" – it was said in a very monotone voice, but she was asking me for something! I quickly came around to the table to ask her what she wanted. "Breakfast" she stated again. I tried to soften my tone, "I know you want breakfast, honey, but what do you want? Pancakes, cereal, toast?"

In a fit of anger, she slapped her hands on the table. "BREAKFAST," she screamed at me again! "I want BREAKFAST." She ran out of the kitchen and so started the 20-minute tantrum. I do not think she ever ate breakfast that day, and I was in tears, again. How was I supposed to know what she wanted for breakfast if she wouldn't tell me? Back to my books and computer to do more research. There had to be something out there that would help me. This is when I first discovered PECS (Picture Exchange System). The basic concept was to place identifying pictures for the child to choose from to help make decisions. The cards were expensive and I was not even sure it would work, so I came up a plan. I began to cut pictures out of magazines: toast, waffles, cereal, sandwiches, chicken, fruit, etc. were all placed on index cards. Every morning they were laid out on the table so she could choose one and communicate effectively on her choice of food for that morning.

I glued them onto index cards and sat with her each day for a week reciting the following mantra: "This is cereal; it is breakfast. This is toast; it is breakfast. This is a sandwich; it is lunch. This is chicken; it is dinner."

Then the day of the test came! She ran downstairs and sat in her favorite chair with the placemat perfectly perpendicular to her body and uttered those all too familiar words, "I want breakfast!" I calmly walked over to the table and placed the index cards in front of her with the breakfast choices. She looked at each card, and handed me the *cereal* card. "I want breakfast."

The end of morning tantrums over food, the beginning of a new way to communicate.

Picture Schedules

The simple act of being able to choose food from pictures became the first step in our daily picture schedules.

Since transitioning was another one of our mountains to climb, staying home often seemed the easiest thing to do. But as you all know, life must go on. There is shopping to do, outdoor work, and shuffling her brother to and from school and sports. None of this was ever done with ease until the schedule!

For anyone battling these types of issues, even if your child has language, the picture schedule is what helps them organize their world. For some reason, when they see it laid out in pictures, they can visualize their day, their transitions, and what is expected. One word of caution – do not add any stops or steps to that schedule on a whim as it will surely spell disaster.

Sample of picture schedule using Mayer-Johnson,
Writing With Symbols 2000 software program

Social Stories

Social Stories became our next step in the language process. As she began to grasp language and schedules, some of our reliance on these items became less and less necessary. Instead of a daily schedule with every step laid out, we could do a more general weekly schedule. Inserting things here and there became possible as she grew older. But social stories became of utmost importance during those elementary years when we were headed out for a big event.

My best explanation of how a social story worked was the day we went to Six Flags® Great America, a theme park in Gurnee, Illinois. It was going to be myself, my husband, Vicky, and her brother, as well as some very close friends of ours.

As we walked through the crowded amusement park entrance, she had in her grasp a copy of her social story for the day. It started out something like this:

> *The lines will be very long.*
> *We will have to wait.*
> *It will be hot outside; you will be sweaty.*
> *If you need a break, you have to ask, not cry and scream.*
> *We will go on the water rides. We will get wet.*
> *We will be so wet, our underwear will be wet, and our shoes will be soggy. We will go on all the water rides and after we are done. We will change into dry clothes. We will not be wet anymore.*

On our first ride, the lines were long. It was a fast open roller coaster that has you diving and doing turns where you feel like you are going to fall out of the car! She clung onto the social story and as she got caught up between all the people, I could hear her reciting to herself, "The line is long, we have to wait...we have to wait...we have to wait."

It was as if by looking at the pictures in her book and saying the words over and over again, she would will herself to make it work. Guess what? It did – she stood in line and was so excited by being on the ride she wanted to do it again!

We caught our mojo for the day! For each ride, for each situation, we had a page in her book to guide her through it. It took me days to decide what to write in this book and what to include, but I was so proud of myself!

Next was the water rides! We read through the pages again about how wet we would get. You see, whenever even a drop of water got on her clothes, she had to change, or just strip down to nothing! That is why this part of the social story was so crucial to the day. It explained how wet she would get and how we would change when it was all over. As the anticipation began, we watched and laughed at all the people coming off the rides, drenched to the bone. We watched the log cars dive into the water with a great splash and listened to her giggle! As we approached the ride, she was so intent at looking up that she stepped into a giant puddle in the walkway.

Anyone standing near us felt the shockwaves. The treacherous scream and then the flying shoe – "My foot is wet, my foot is wet," she screamed in a tortured voice! We found her shoe and scooped her up and pulled her to the side to calm her down.

I had to be out of my mind to even think about her going on these water rides. But when I asked if she still wanted to go on them, through her sobs was an emphatic YES! You see, getting wet on the rides was predetermined in the social story – stepping in the puddle was not. And just when I was patting myself on the back for being so prepared…

A funny side note to this story is the "Vicky Pass". You see we learned that we could get a handicapped pass for her. Yes, I know what you are thinking, and let me tell you did we get the looks. She does not look physically challenged and when we went up to the handicapped line, people would give us a look. But waiting in line was torture for her. I thought that she should be allowed to enjoy her day without feeling the agony of everyone touching her and bumping into her. Her cousins really got into the idea because they got to bump the line with her. And hence the name, the "Vicky Pass!"

When we traveled to Florida during spring break – I wrote her a social story on how long the car ride would take (too long if you ask me!). And what stops we would make, and what we would do when we arrived. I also put down that while we were in the car, she was not allowed to complain, cry or fight with her brother. When we made a scheduled hotel stop to sleep before continuing on, when we got into the hotel room, she immediately began fighting with her brother. I was tired and the last thing I needed to hear was both of them complaining so I reminded Vicky of her social story. She took a breather from her argument with her brother and told me (in an "I quote" tone of voice), "The story says we can't fight in the car – we're not in the car!" A quick little edit of the book took care of future fights

CHAPTER 7

STANDARDIZED TESTING

For anyone with a child on the spectrum, you are probably aware of how exhausting standardized testing is. With Common Core, it seems like a never ending stream of testing for the students in school. The stress of this testing is not just hard on the students, but on parents and teachers as well.

George W. Bush

You are probably reading this right now and wondering what George Bush and my daughter have in common. A few minutes of indulgence, please....

It was the beginning of second grade (2004) and election season. Bush was making his run for his second term as president and so his name was often in the news. My daughter was in regular classes with support. Here in Illinois it was time for the MAP tests. It was agreed upon in her I.E.P. (Individual Education Plan) set the year before that the test would only be administered until the point of frustration.

The first day of the testing, her resource teacher walked her out after school and looked as harried as I have felt. She explained that testing did not go well, and she was ready to stop, but the principal of the school felt that she needed to try and finish out the rest of the tests. I took Vicky home and mulled over whether I wanted to push her into completing these tests. She was in a grouchy mood and was very withdrawn. When I tried to ask her about the tests she told me they were stupid and cried and sobbed and asked over and over why she had to take these tests. I knew I had to answer this question because she was demanding an answer. Enter George Bush! I explained to her that George Bush has to test the schools to see if they are teaching properly, and the only way for him to know this was if each student took one of these tests. Only then, by the student's scores, would his office know if the teachers were teaching properly.

She dried her tears. "George Bush thinks I should take this test?" she asked me again. I nodded. She wiped her tears and walked away, saying nothing. As many parents of children with autism find out on their journey, rule following is crucial to them. So, if the President of the United States said she had to take the test, well, she knew she had to follow the rules.

We had a day in between testing, so we were able to brainstorm on some techniques that would help her concentrate. The teacher discovered she liked a fan blowing right on her face and at home we always listened to Mozart when doing our homework (The Mozart Effect), so I sent in her tapes. She also got to sit on a ball chair and have the lights turned down a little.

Well, low and behold, she finished the entire week of testing! I will not discuss the scores because it will only lead me on another tangent on how standardized tests are not necessarily an indication of our children's knowledge. Testing does not always take into consideration the alternate processing skills many of our children share. At any rate, she finished the test. When it came time for ISAT (Illinois State Achievement Testing) in early spring, she was distraught once more – this time, I told her the governor needed these results and she took them with no complaints.

CHAPTER 8

AUTISM: THE PRE-TEEN YEARS

The school district my kids attended has a separate building for 5th and 6th grade and then another building for 7th and 8th grade. The move from her safe and caring elementary school was a big one for both of us. I had begun working as a teaching assistant in the same district so I could have the same schedule as she did. She had a wonderful team in 5th grade, and she seemed to do well. It was still easy at this point to make play dates for her, but I often remember I would be the one entertaining the girls. She also became a girl scout and I thought this would be an excellent opportunity for her to make friends. It worked for a while, but she always seemed to enjoy spending time with the leader instead of the girls. It was not until years later that she told me she always felt left out from the other girls. It was the beginning the "girl world" for her and it would not be a pleasant journey.

Sixth grade was by far one of her worst years. She struggled with the emerging friendships of girls moving into pre-teens and positioning for "cool" status. She had a special education teacher who was in her last year of teaching before retirement and was worn out. She made my daughter feel stupid, although I did not know that until the end of the year. Her tests scores continued to lag and she was always identified by the state as below average or at academic warning. We often refer to these years as the "lost years." She hated being pulled for testing, she hated being moved into small groups, and she made sure she told me every day. I always felt I was doing the right thing, so I continued to push her through and tell her that she needed this extra attention because she needed additional help. I did not realize that a big storm was brewing.

Seventh Grade

Up until this point, I had allowed her IEP to dictate her classes and her placement. But my job as a teaching assistant had taught me some new skills and allowed me to observe education from a different side. I realized that she was now at the precipice of her education. Up until this point, I had always walked through every assignment with her. I helped her plan, ran out and got the best supplies for projects, and argued through homework. Sometimes, I even put the words in her mouth when she was writing because I wanted her to be successful. Then, one day as I was helping students in a science class, the teacher told me I was helping too much. In a nice way, she told me to back off and let the students struggle. It was through their own work they would learn to be successful. Mind you, I was in my late 40's at this point and this teacher had not yet hit her 30th birthday. I was a little put off at the moment, and felt it was my job to make sure the kids were successful in their classes. Besides, what could this teacher possibly know about how some of these students struggled. I wrestled with my emotions about wanting to help these kids succeed and knowing they needed to learn things on their own. Then, it hit me. If I gave them the answers, they would never learn to stand on their own two feet. Had I helped my own daughter too much? Was I hurting her more than helping her? Oh, those times of reassessing whether or not you are being a good parent. Every day I questioned if what I was doing was the right thing. Every day, I waffled between letting her struggle and helping make things easier in a world that was already so difficult for her. So when she got to 7th grade, I requested she get put on the team with the very teacher who told me I helped too much. And so the best and worst year began simultaneously.

What is "Sad" and how a Simile saved me!

By this time, my daughter had been playing trumpet for two years with the 5th and 6th grade band. Music was fun for her and when she got into the middle school building, the band was big and did performed in all sorts of competitions. As a former band member myself, I knew she was enjoying playing her music, but it also gave me another difficult choice. Band was during study hall, but she needed reading interventions as well. I was in the reading department and knew the skills she needed to learn were important. I also knew how much music meant to her. I made the decision every IEP team hates - I would not let her go to interventions. Here I was, one of the teaching assistants that helped kids with reading skills every day, and I had decided NOT to let my own daughter, with a below average reading level, take interventions because I thought band was more important. My daughter was elated; my teacher friends not so much. Yet, because I was in the reading department, I knew I could help my daughter with her homework like a teacher - not a parent. I did not give her the answers, I guided her. She had no pull out classes this year. I decided I would rather her get a C in a class that was truly her C, then an A with so much guidance that she did not have to do her work. I asked the teachers to make her take her own notes. I only supplied her with the finished ones when she had a chance to work on her own. I co-read every book she read so that we could discuss it and talk about the characters and the plot. We watched movies together and I pointed out character traits and plot lines and story settings.

Then, one day she came home quite distraught. She was writing a narrative and had used the word "sad" in her paper. Her teacher had done an edit and told her that she needed a more descriptive word that just "sad." Well, if you can imagine the literal mind of a child with autism, this request was not okay. She raged on to me about how silly it was that her teacher did not understand the word "sad." Who doesn't know what "sad" means and why on earth would she be expected to explain it! I was at a loss. I thought her paper was one of the best things she had written, and this LA teacher was telling her the word "sad" was not good enough. I was a little miffed at this teacher myself. Why couldn't she understand putting feelings down on paper was especially hard for my daughter. With a stubborn 12-year-old not willing to write anything else but "sad" because she felt the request was stupid, and wanting to help her edit her paper, I sought the advice of the reading specialist. And that is when a SIMILE saved the day! I got a chance to ask my daughter if she was "sad" like she had spilled her milk or "sad" like her dog died. I tried to explain that although they were both "sad" one was far worse than the other. She took her paper, reread the line where she was "sad." Without saying a word, she added "sad as a flower that someone forgot to water." The teacher was thrilled and my daughter had learned a new way to express herself.

8th Grade and A 10,000 Word Story

In 8th grade, her LA teacher challenged all the students to write a 10,000-word fiction story. I never knew that her world could be so creative. It was fun to watch her develop characters and settings and plot lines from her view of life with autism. It was a shining moment for her and for us. I realized that perhaps the years of doing the *Mozart Effect* and signing her up for drama when she was younger had finally paid off. What I was not prepared for was the drama of the teen years that were just around the corner.

Enter, Billie Joe Armstrong

Billie Joe Armstrong…. this was not a new name to our household. Just seven years earlier, my son had discovered the band **Green Day** and its lead singer. I remember the first CD I purchased for my son - I think the album was called "Dookie" - and it was one of the first CD's with the new parental warning labels.

My son was always a level-headed kid, so although I did not really approve of the language on the CD, I felt that he was old enough to understand not to use the language - at least around adults. Several years later, my daughter discovered music through her IPod. She listened to Disney recordings, Hannah Montana, and other songs that were parent approved. And then Billie Joe entered our lives again. *Green Day* had become one of her favorite bands. I was horrified that at age eight or nine she was listening to such raw music. I listened and learned every word from *21st Century Breakdown* to *American Idiot.* Many of my family members and friends chastised me for letting her listen to this music. It was not even a ploy to let her listen to things her peer group were listening to. Green Day was an older band with no new albums at this point. She just really enjoyed the music. With the invention of Google, I found her watching YouTube videos, and asking for books documenting Billie Joe's life. She studied every lyric and knew where the songs came from - deep in the emotions of a young man who never quite fit in.

Feeling her differences was apparently what sparked her interest in this punk rock star. The older she became the more alienated from her so called "friends" she became. She struggled with self-image, hormones came into play, and I saw the face of anxiety and depression come into focus. No stranger to that black hole that wants to suck you in, I got her into a therapist as quickly as possible. Teen years with girls can be stormy, I remember my own with my mother, but there was more to this. One night, a fight began for what reason I cannot even remember….and then it happened. She dropped the "F" bomb on her parents. Convinced that Billie Joe was to blame for this, I snatched up all of her *Green Day* CD's (she had the full collection thanks to her brother), and took away the IPod. Did you hear the beginning of World War III, because Ground Zero was at my house?

Once again I questioned my sanity - why did I allow her to listen to this music? Did it make her darker, make her feel less loved? We had always shared every moment together, I was there through all the toddler rage, but there was no comparison to this teen rage which also came with the words, "I wish I were dead".

Being a Girl with Autism

My daughter specifically asked me to write a section on how hard it was for me to find groups with girls. According to the Autism Society in 2014, 1 in every 68 births will result in a child being diagnosed with autism. The CDC reports that "ASD is about 4.5 times more common among boys (1 in 42) than among girls (1 in 189)" (http://www.cdc.gov/ncbddd/autism/data.html). What that meant for my daughter is that groups that were dedicated to help with social situations with people on the spectrum were geared more towards boys. And while I am not making any scientific generalizations, many of the boy's groups seemed to focus on video games, Minecraft, technology, trains, etc. None of the things that interested my daughter. So what happened was she did not fit in with the neurotypical group of girls who played with dolls, listened to music, had fun dressing up and playing with make-up but she didn't fit in with the boys in the autism groups either. It made her life very lonely at times, and although she really never complained, I know now that it was hard for her.

Perhaps someday there will be groups that work toward bringing together social situations for girls on all ends of the spectrum so they may share camaraderie with their age group, or learn to mentor younger girls.

CHAPTER 9

MODERN MEDICINE RESCUES US AGAIN

I have never been an advocate of medicating kids with pills. Therapy was helping, but my daughter's level of anxiety and depression was too much and I was not going to let her drown. With a doctor's recommendation in hand, we went for the next level of help. She came around to become the level-headed girl I knew she could be, once her medication took effect. She still deals with anxiety and depression, but knows how to work through things. And, Billie Joe was let back into our lives. We saw the stage performance of *American Idiot,* I took her to their *99 Revolutions* concert, after the fateful meltdown of Billie Joe on stage at the *I Heart Radio* concert. Although I still am not a fan of the language used in the albums of *Green Day*, the tunes are catchy; I respect where they came from, and I love that my daughter "hears" the message in every song. She has attended "Warped Tour" for the past four years and I even took her to a "Panic! At the Disco" concert a few years back.

Her love of music showed when we visited the Rock N Roll Hall of Fame in Cleveland, Ohio. Her knowledge and appreciation for music is one that not every young person experiences. Like every parent who lets their children play violent video games and wonders if that is okay, I too questioned myself on allowing her to listen to this music. I understand that music calms her. So, my advice to parents struggling with the same issues is to make sure you engage with your child and his or her activities. Discuss the realities and fantasies. This advice holds true for neuro-typical children as well.

CHAPTER 10

AUTISM: HIGH SCHOOL

The move to high school was exciting. There would be new friends to make, teachers who did not know her and new challenges for her to face. She was going to join the high school band, and was excited and nervous to start marching band. She did well in her classes, met some new friends, and it looked like it was going to be a good setting for her to flourish.

The summer after her Freshman year, I decided to let her take the school trip to the United Kingdom. This trip was not tied to an AP (Advanced Placement) class and they were fine taking a student with an I.E.P. on the trip. She had to go to class one Sunday each month for five hours starting in January and she received a semester credit in history. The class studied the cultures of the countries they would visit. They also studied the history and the literature. The group would travel to Ireland, Scotland, Wales, and England for ten days right after she finished her freshman year. I was hopeful it would help her become more independent because she would have to take care of her possessions, carry her bags, and take care of her money. She needed to obtain a passport, get a bank account with a debit card, and put on a credit card. She would be unable to bring any electronics with her - no phone, no computer. The only piece of electronic gear she carried was a Kindle so she could read and blog, and of course her beloved music on her iPod.

No problem, I thought to myself, and we started to teach her about the exchange rate for Pounds and Euros. We made a cheat sheet of approximately what she would be spending. If something cost 10 Euros, then it would be \$11.31 if the exchange rate stayed static. We converted money in Euros and Pounds before she left so she could have available cash with her in the countries she would travel. We packed clothes and matched outfits. We taught her how to pack with luggage cubes to keep her clothes organized. She was busy writing papers, learning to bake Irish soda bread and make potato soup. She finished her Freshman year making the honor roll, and a few days later my husband and I were standing in the school parking lot as the kids loaded up their bags on a bus and headed off the airport. I waved to the 22 students and four teachers that would be chaperoning them in four countries over the next ten days. And then the homonym of the word "wave" hit me like a tsunami! What was I thinking? I just put my 15-year-old daughter with autism on a bus with four teachers that I had little to no true contact with, and 21 other students that ranged from sophomores to seniors in high school. None of these students were truly her friends, as this issue was still difficult for her. I felt sick to my stomach. This wave of terror hit me – what if something did not go well, I had no way to help her - I did not even have a current passport!

Well, of course, she pulled through with flying colors. The teachers kept Twitter accounts and every picture I saw of her, she was smiling and having a great time. When she returned, I looked at her pictures, and realized that although I was terrified at first, this trip did more for her self-esteem that anything I could have ever done for her.

They had to keep a photo journal and the trip I saw through her eyes still amazes me. From castles to flowers, from food to friends, I got to glimpse her trip through her photographs. I framed pictures of flowers she took at one of the castles, and she even won an honorable mention in a photography contest at the local county fair. Her experiences were broadening, she was experiencing life, and she was happy.

CHAPTER 11

THE ACT AND PREPARING FOR COLLEGE

Her Junior year was upon us before we knew it. It is the toughest year for almost any high schooler because of the pressure to do well in classes for the GPA which is reported to colleges. It is also the year of the ACT. When she finished her sophomore year, I had her take the test blindly, so that she could get over the stress of it. No accommodations, no extra time, just to take the test and understand what she needed to study. Her score: a 14. Okay, so now we know what we have to do. I signed her up for the ACT class at school. I did not sign her up for one of those expensive classes because she was mad at the testing world. You see, since she was little she has been in the "academic warning" part of grading. She cannot take standardized tests. If I could reword all the questions for her, then we would be fine, but of course reading tests are not allowed any accommodations, so she had to tough through this part on her own. After taking the ACT class at school, she took several practice tests and still got a 14. We set up another ACT test where she took it over three days, since sometimes extra time on test day prolongs the agony. Guess what - she got a 15! She even agreed to try the SAT - thinking it might be written a little differently. When she received her test results – you got it - it equaled a 15!

Many of the colleges that we visited told us that the ACT was not the only thing they used for admission. Do not believe it. The reality of it is, a 17 is about the lowest score most colleges will even consider, even if they say they do not require the ACT. We were fortunate the

39

University of Dubuque decided to do a personal interview to meet her and see if she was college material. Her admissions advisor was supportive and the Dean of Freshman Admissions talked with her candidly. When he realized how hard she had tried to get a higher score on her test, he moved on to look at her grades (3.4 GPA), her extracurricular and volunteer work, and offered her admission into their Bridge Program which would help her become a college student. Her first year was a success, and once again she proved she could do it. I knew my job was to continually search for the best resources to help my child.

The beginning of her junior year started out happy. Although she did not have any close friends, she seemed content. She made it through the ACT and applied for college. Then the worst thing ever happened: she got bullied in the place that she loved the most – band. I was always amazed at her ability to play her instrument and march – this takes lots of coordination, and with her sensory issues, to watch her perform in a 140+ piece band took my breath away. She always tried so hard, but this particular year, the music was difficult and she was having trouble keeping up with the choreography. One of her section mates, a senior student, had no patience with her and began to bully her. She tried to address it with her teachers, but did not get much support. Her normal happy self was deteriorating before our eyes. She dreaded band and she dreaded school. I did not know it then, but this would be her last year in high school band.

Senior Year

Senior year would be the year she dropped band. The stress of being bullied was too much and even the promise of a trip to New York to march in the Veterans' Day Parade was no enticement to continue. Sad to see her lay down her trumpet after seven years, I had an idea. Our community college has a concert band and anyone could join. There were no try outs - just show up! This would be great - she could still play. One catch - because she was not yet eighteen, an adult would have to accompany her. So, guess what I did! I played French horn during high school, college, and in the alumni band - 20 years ago. Hey, it has got to be like riding a bike, right? So out came Pierre (my nickname for my French horn - get it? Pierre??). It was like riding a bike. Once I got the stampede of elephants out of the instrument, my daughter and I had two semesters of band together. What a rush to sit on stage and feel like a college kid myself, with my daughter sitting right behind me in the trumpet section. I almost wanted to call the band director and the kid that bullied her and thank them for giving me the gift of being in weekly rehearsals with my daughter. Nothing could have been more special.

Senior year continued with the usual events. There was homecoming, prom, and lots of studying. She took a Public Service Practicum (PSP) class that led her to volunteer work in several different places. She got her driver's license that year as well, and I was beginning to realize I needed to let go. The day she wore her cap and gown was such a proud moment for my family, and especially for me. High school was over; she was not leaving old friends, she was not leaving an abundance of teachers who really cared for her, she was leaving behind what had felt like agony to her and was getting a new beginning.

CHAPTER 12

College

The summer before college moved quickly. She worked as a henna tattoo artist at Great America and we shopped and prepared for her move to Dubuque, Iowa. It was a bittersweet moment when we moved her stuff into her dorm room. We did all of the Freshman activities, and then we pulled away, waving good bye while she stood in front of her dorm building. I remember doing the same for my son, and I remember crying the entire way home. The tears for my daughter, however, were so very different. I had raised this child and stood by her side every day. I taught her to manage her time, to handle her tantrums, to express her emotions, to play, and to live. I was now being asked to let go. It was time to see if all I had taught her was going to work. I worried every day. I would call her to check on her, and she was so determined to do everything herself, that she would barely talk to me. I remember one time calling her, just wanting to hear her voice, and she answered her phone, "I can't talk to you right now, I am busy!" She hung up the phone. I realize now that it was her way of dealing with our separation. We had always been "best friends" in a lot of ways, and I think we missed each other more than we could admit.

So many years ago, the doctors gave me no real hope, no real guidance. And yet, here she was making her way on a college campus. There are no IEPs in college. There are limited accommodations, but the truth of the matter is, college is the next step to independent life. She made it through the first year of her business degree tackling classes like macro and microeconomics, algebra, and World View Seminar with a 3.2

GPA. As she continues her journey through college, she still has a long road ahead of her to complete independence. She has made new friends, took the car, and even found a part time job. I hold my breath every day as I learn to live my life again, without autism. But for my daughter, living without autism will never be her reality. Each day she lives her life under the influence autism. Some days it will make her life hard, other days it may enrich her life because of the sense of perception that it gives her. I can only hope that what lies ahead will be filled with kind and understanding people, and that her tenacity and love of success will carry her through even the darkest times.

PART II

LOOKING AT LIFE FROM THE OTHER SIDE

By Victoria A. Kulig

CHAPTER 13

Autism: The Younger Years From the Other Side

I do remember the happy times I had when I was little, but sometimes the horrible ones take over. I remember the first day of preschool. I was balling my eyes out because I missed my mom and thought she didn't love me because she would leave me in this strange place. I remember crying so hard I couldn't catch my breath. I just remember every teacher screaming "VICKY, IT'S OKAY." To me, it was flat out screaming, and they were not comforting me. My mom says those teachers were a blessing, but I thought differently.

When we moved back to Illinois in 2001, my brother and I were starting at new schools. I remember I was in the morning kindergarten class but I always felt out of sync with the rest of the kids and I noticed I was different from the other kids. I would try to play with them, but they didn't like to play with me or I just didn't understand what they were doing. I thought they hated me. After morning kindergarten, I went to daycare, and I hated every minute. Every single kid was very mean to me, or at least that is how it felt, so I just went off and played by myself. Even when playing by myself, I felt the kids were still mean to me, always watching me, always judging me. That was my "normal."

When first grade started, I thought I was going to be normal, in classes with no special aides. But that didn't turn out the way I liked it either. I was in pull-out classes with kids I didn't like or want to be friends with. I kept telling my teachers that I wanted to be in the regular room, with the regular kids. They just kept saying "no" and brushed me off. I wanted to be challenged and I felt my teachers didn't believe in me. I was very frustrated. Finally, around 2nd or 3rd grade, I asked my mom, "What's wrong with me?" I wanted to know why was I being pulled out and why I was not with the regular kids? She told me I had autism and tried to explain what it was. I think that was the moment I was determined not to be in the pull out groups anymore. I knew I didn't belong there and I wanted bigger and better things.

In 4th and 5th grade, I made sure to stand up for myself with what I wanted and to be sure everyone heard me. The adults were sometimes taken back by what I did or said, but it was the only way I could make myself heard. By 7th grade, I was finally mainstreamed; no pull out classes and no interventions.

Friendships are complicated, no matter who you are. But for me, it felt like World War III. I used to think, *This should be so simple, why is it so hard for me?*" Again, it never seemed like the other kids really liked me that much. To compound things, all of the summer camps I went to were special needs camps, and because autism affects girls at a lesser rate, I was always the only girl with all boys. So I spent most of my time with the female counselors because that was the only thing that was feminine.

CHAPTER 14

The Teen Years
From the Other Side

My mom titles this section, "**Enter Billie Joe Armstrong,**" I call this stage my "emo" stage. I wanted to be my own person and I liked the reaction I got by listening to this music. I was doing something that my parents didn't like, and it felt good. The reason I loved Green Day so much was because they were total outcasts in their teens. I felt I was the outcast, referred to as a "the stupid girl" in school, or at least that was what I thought. I knew from the very beginning that I was very different from the other kids. My mom details the fight and me dropping the "F" bomb. Concerning the fight with my parents? I do not remember what the fight was exactly about, but I do remember the adrenaline running through me and hearing mixed signals from my parents. That four letter word - it just came out. I didn't mean it, it just happened. I still think to this day the way my parents handled this situation was not really fair. What I did was wrong, and I do not blame my parents for being extremely angry at me, but music is my life and when they took it away, I was crushed. I questioned my sanity after that. I realized without music, I was nothing. I wish I could press rewind and changed my actions and maybe talk about what I was feeling at the moment. Rather than just taking my music away, my parents could have handled it differently. I felt I was not in my own body. It was as if this monster was controlling me, and I wanted it to stop, but it couldn't make it stop. Sometimes, that is what autism feels like - this rush of emotion that you just cannot stop in its tracks.

CHAPTER 15

Autism: High School From the Other Side

Oh, high school, where kids are starting to determine who they are as a person. I honestly believed the teachers at orientation when they said that high school was the best four years of our lives, but they were wrong! There is no doubt that I have some wonderful memories, but many of them were not so wonderful. A good memory? I got to go to Ireland and the UK when I was 15, without my parents! Then, in my sophomore year, the high school marching band took a trip to Walt Disney World. The band marched in the Magic Kingdom Electrical Parade and our band played to a scene in the *Lion King*. But, as always, that social awkwardness always followed me. I went to high school with the kids from my middle school and I think they still thought of me as stupid and weird and it was rubbing off on new people whom I did not know that well.

Being Bullied

Fast forward to my junior year. I think junior year is one of the toughest years yet. People are studying for ACT/SATs and trying to figure out if they're going to college or what are they going to do. But my junior year was the darkest year of my life. To start off, I had a brand new case manager. He was in his mid-to-late 20's, and I thought he was trying too hard, but my mom really liked him, at first. Marching band was starting to get really intense, it felt like I was getting ready for combat not a football game. Up until this point, although I always felt other kids didn't like me or relate to me, I never felt bullied. But was junior year was when I encountered my first bullying situation. This guy got mad whenever I would accidently run into him on the practice field, but it only happened the first two days when we would learn a new routine. He was a senior and I had looked up to him before this, but every day he acted so irritated with me and instead of helping me he seemed to be making fun of me. Finally, one day he yelled at me, "MOVE OR I'LL CHOP YOUR F**ING HEAD OFF!!" I stood there in shock, my was confidence ripped to shreds. One girl who saw it happen told me just let it go, that was just how he dealt with his anger. I told my mom about the incident and she immediately emailed my teachers to find out about the situation. My band director was in such disbelief, she thought I was making the story up. I had always respected my teachers before that point, but I lost my respect at that moment – the band director didn't support me, and my case manager advised me to "forget it". I thought to myself, "*How could I get such lack of support from teachers, of all people?!*" Was I crazy? What was wrong with me? It was obvious to me they cared more about winning competitions and taking care of their favorite students. This incident robbed me of my dignity and made me feel very unsure of myself, and still haunts me today.

Friend Intervention

Second semester got really intense, everybody was getting ready to take the ACT and I was at the boiling point. I was still in band which was still intense. Although marching season was over, it was now concert time. I was in the advanced band, but I was last chair with two freshmen ahead of me. I always felt like no one really saw me. I took private trumpet lessons and practiced, but still never seemed to be good enough. Having two freshmen put in chair above me was the cherry on top. Like I said, I pretty much went to school with people whom I've known since first grade and I do not think people realized how much I had gone through and how much I had changed. I was taught, however, to try and stick things out. So, even in the bad situations I went to school every day and participated in band, hating every moment.

51

On top of everything else, my case worker was on a mission to make sure that I was able to make friends. There was another girl, who I had known for about ten years, who was diagnosed with Asperger's Syndrome. My case manager also had her on his caseload. He decided that since we both had some form of autism, we needed to be best friends. We both got along with each other but we couldn't really be close friends because we just didn't share that much in common. There were some little incidents that happened, but we were always able to resolve them. Then the day before my 17th birthday, our case manager decided to set up an "intervention," where he told the other girl he would get us together to discuss our differences. I was blindsided!! I did not even know we had differences to get over. I was called to his office, but didn't know why. I found out this intervention was to make me be friends with this girl. Like I said, I did not have that much in common with her and I didn't want to pursue a close friendship. She felt I was not supportive of her and the case manager proceeded to tell me how I always handled things poorly and I felt like he made me look like the bad guy. I brought up the bullying situation and how she witnessed it, but did not support me, and I watched him become very mad at me. I had opened Pandora's Box. The case manager yelled, "HOW COULD YOU BRING THAT UP? THE SITUATION WAS TAKEN CARE OF!!!!" I knew at that moment that I needed to keep my mouth shut. During my lunch break I texted my mom to let her know that the intervention didn't go well. She had no idea what I was talking about. I gave her a brief explanation of what happened over a text and told her that I would talk to her that night. The case manager called to let her know what he was trying to accomplish. He was trying to make it look like he did the right thing and that I reacted poorly. All I know is that my mom's blood was boiling. She felt he had no right to do an intervention of this type without alerting her or my dad. The moral of the story: Do NOT force your kids to be friends with anyone that they choose not to be friends with.

Finally, a Friend

The one thing this case manager did right was to set up a "student sponsoring student" peer program. I got matched up with a girl a year younger than myself, and we went different places during the end of my junior year. That summer, I had the best summer with a friend I had ever experienced. We spent a ton of time together at each other's houses and going to Six Flags® Great America Amusement Park. I met her friends, and hung out with her family. I learned a lot about what being a friend meant. Our friendship didn't last and at first I was really baffled and hurt, but I realize now it was a great learning experience and I will never forget our time of being friends.

CHAPTER 16

College Life
From the Other Side

College has to be one of the best things that has ever happened to me. I said to my high school peers, "*I look forward to never ever seeing you again!*" and I began my new journey. I was saying goodbye to Grayslake, Illinois and hello to Dubuque, Iowa. A new place equals a new start! In the beginning, it was a little rough because I did not know anybody since most of the people were either from Eastern Iowa, Northwest Illinois, or Southwest Wisconsin, but I managed to make really close bonds by forcing myself into things that would take me out of my comfort zone.

Having a roommate for the first time was a great stressor for my parents. At first, they wanted me to have a single room, thinking I would be better off in my own space. But, I was like, "NO!" I wanted the full experience. I wanted a roommate. The room was small, but my roommate was kind. We were not best friends, but we got along. My computer and headphones helped me block out the world and gave me the opportunity to decide when I wanted to be social and when I wanted to be quiet. I learned to invite people into my room and I would walk the hallway looking for open doors if I was lonely. I found the best little local pizza joint to hang out with friends and enjoyed the freedom of being on my own.

One of the best decisions I made so far, was joining Phi Theta Psi, a co-ed fraternity, at the University of Dubuque. When I initially told them that I had autism, they didn't care about the diagnosis, and they didn't think of me as weird, strange, or stupid. I was in tears of happiness because I finally told someone about my diagnosis and they were not judgmental of me; this was the moment that I finally let my guard down to a group of people who were just getting to know me. Thetas are the first group of friends that I have ever had in my entire life who accepted me for me, and not my autism. There are members in Thetas that have been through a lot worse than I have, but can say "*I know how you feel*" and can do something to make me feel better. I can say that they have become my family, I would do anything for any of them, and I know that they would return the favor.

I was also lucky enough to be part of two programs that help students acclimate to college life and career life. The first program was The Bridge program offered by UD. This program helped teach me how to be a college student. There were mandatory study sessions and professors who helped me navigate the new adult world that college offered.

The other program was the Trio program. I heard about this program through the Bridge Program and decided to pursue being a part of this group. I had to interview and apply to see if you were accepted. I have made a commitment to the program to attend seminars, additional advising, and tutoring to help me navigate my way from college life to adulthood. I also received scholarships for my grades through this program. I am particularly proud of this accomplishment because I did it all by myself - my parents didn't even know I was applying this program.

But do not let this success fool you. Life on the spectrum is still hard. I tried to do things without support and lost my footing. I realized that not just people with autism need help and support – everyone does. This may be the hardest part for me – trying to show people I can accomplish anything and still ask for help. I hope that as I continue to move into adult life I can figure out how to balance this concept.

CHAPTER 17

Looking Ahead
From the Other Side

I realize now that my autism does not define me. The next chapters of my life are because I am a human being, NOT a human being with autism. I expect that my life will have ups and downs just like everyone else's. I realize that I may always struggle socially, but now I know how to choose friends who can help support me instead of just making me feel stupid.

I recently helped mentor a young man who was going into his junior year of high school. I remember him saying "Thanks for making me realize there are colleges for people like us." My reply was, "What are you, an alien? Last I checked we are human." I realize that I used to define myself by my autism. I now define myself as being part of the crazy human race.

In the words of Gerard Way of *My Chemical Romance*, this is what I like to live by:

Do or die you'll never make me
'Cause the world, will never take my heart
Though you try, you'll never break me
We want it all, we wanna play this part

Won't explain or say I'm sorry
I'm not ashamed, I'm gonna show my scar
Give a cheer for all the broken.

(Permission granted from My Chemical Romance,
Lyrics from Black Parade)

The
Simple Way
to Start the
GF/CF Diet

An Easy Guide to Implementing
the Gluten Free/Casein Free Diet
for Your Child with Autism

by Natalie A. Kulig

PART III

THE DIET

The following section of this book was first published as

The Simple Way to Start the GF/CF Diet

An easy guide to implementing the Gluten Free/
Casein Free Diet for your Child with Autism

It was originally published 2008, 2009 and is presented with updates.

INCORPORATING GLUTEN FREE/CASEIN FREE FOOD INTO EVERYDAY LIFE

Just thinking about beginning the Gluten Free/Casein Free Diet is overwhelming. I remember first hearing about the diet just shortly after my then 3-year-old daughter was diagnosed with Autism. There was an article written by Karyn Serousi in *Parents Magazine* about how she cured her son's autism with this Gluten Free/Casein Free Diet.

I read it and dismissed it—I was not going to start taking things out of my child's diet without even understanding what this diagnosis meant to my daughter or my family.

And so, my long journey began. Each of us handles the diagnosis of Autism in a different way. At first, it is hard to accept. Then we need to blame someone or something. Then we accept. What we do during this time, however, is critical.

Because I am a researcher by nature, I began my journey the day I received her diagnosis. The team of doctors and therapists who diagnosed her sent me home with handfuls of information, articles and therapy options. I read many of the medical articles and was confused as to what my daughter might need. I had heard about ABA (applied behavioral analysis), supplements, occupational therapy and diet treatments. I chose the path of somewhat "alternative" medicine looking to a chiropractor for initial help. I started my journey at a center in Louisville, Kentucky, called the **Kentuckiana Children's Center.** They concentrated on children with special needs. It was here that I learned some of the things that I believe have profoundly helped my daughter.

My intention in this section is not to give you information about the science and etiology of how gluten and casein are in tolerated as there are many more scientific books out there to help explain the details. My intention is to help guide you through some of the information and how to use it. What we do with our children is extremely personal—from how we discipline to what therapies we use. Plus, anyone with a child on the spectrum knows that it is so large; there is no "one size fits all" remedy.

THE DIET – FROM THE OTHER SIDE

When I first started the diet, I remember the kids at school looking at me like I was a little weird. My food was different, I had my own treat bag at school, and could not eat the yummy birthday treats the other kids brought in to share. I remember my mom trying to get me to eat things that tasted like paper, and people at restaurants looked at us like we were crazy when we asked for a burger without a bun. Today, none of this would be a problem. I can go to the nicest restaurants and get gluten free pasta, I can order gluten free buns, and even get gluten free desserts.

Although I might not stick to my diet as much as my mom would like me to, I have found over the years, I can tolerate small bits of gluten and casein without it making me feel different. But I always know when I have had too much. I feel like I want to pull into my own world and socializing becomes more difficult. So, sometimes when I gluten overload, I just need to be gluten free and casein for a few days, drink a lot of water, and cocoon until I feel better.

I know this diet affects everyone differently, and even though a lot of people thought my mom was crazy, I am grateful she made me do it, because I did feel better and was able to be more social.

FIRST STEPS TO UNDERSTANDING
THE PURPOSE OF THE DIET

I believe the first step to implementing the diet is to read Karyn Serousi's book, *Unraveling the Mystery of Autism and Pervasive Development Disorders.* It will give you the background of all her research and how she uncovered what different foods and their proteins could do to the body. When I read what gluten and casein could do to the body and mind of a child with autism, I was amazed. I was also astounded by the effect of apples, bananas and other fruits that contained high amounts of natural phenol sulfates and the opiate-like effect it could have on the brain. I started my daughter on the diet in July of 2000 – she was three years old at the time. The effects have been profound. The diet was not a cure, but I believe it helped her feel better making her therapies work more efficiently. After 14 years on the diet, she makes her own food choices and knows what she can and cannot have. I believe that the earlier the diet intervention, the easier time the child will have making this a life-long habit.

The first time she emerged from her own little autistic world and asked me to play, I cried. When she looked up at the sky while on vacation, she noted all the "sheep" in the blue sky (the clouds). While we take for granted these small gestures in our normal developing children, we are amazed and rewarded when our child with autism make these milestones.

I was once at a lecture about the GF/CF diet and there was a doctor who tried to explain, in lay terms, what the diet was about and how it may help our children. Here is a brief synopsis on why the diet works. This was explanation I used to inform friends, family and school personnel so they understood WHY my daughter could not have these foods.

> *Your body takes all food it digests in the stomach. From there, the food proteins are broken down into peptides. Then, they are broken down one more level into amino acids. These amino acids are released into the bloodstream and are used by the body.*
>
> *In the case of many children with Autism, their bodies have what is called a "leaky gut". This means that the peptides get into the bloodstream before they are broken down into amino acids and the body does not know how to use them. They begin to clog up the body's own system and many neurotransmitters to the brain are blocked or clogged as well."*
>
> *Wheat and dairy proteins seem to be the biggest offenders, although often times, corn and soy may also be culprits, each child is unique. This also explains why, if your child does respond positively to the diet it is as if a fog has lifted and everything becomes clearer.*

This was the case with my child. She went from barely speaking words, throwing tantrums and screaming to get what she needed, to speaking in two to three word sentences. A year and a half later, she became fully verbal.

Autism is a complex condition and no two children are alike. It is my belief that the diet is a good place to start finding answers. Even with many medical doctors discrediting the diet, I still felt it was worth the time and effort. Even the smallest gain – not stimming, talking, moving through a schedule – is so rewarding. The most important thing to remember is you need to give it time to work. Your child may not respond immediately – and it is an all or nothing effort – a little milk or wheat is like giving a diabetic a little sugar or forgetting one shot – it is a big deal – you must make a commitment.

Now it is time to look into the workings of the diet.

Keep in mind that if you decide to do this diet…

- It will be difficult
- You will make many, many mistakes,
- Depending on the age of your child, you may not see immediate results. It may take weeks or months,
- Your grocery bill will go up,
- You will become a connoisseur of ingredients you never heard of,
- It will become easier as time goes on.

Step 1: Take Out the Diary

The first and easiest step is to take out milk and dairy. What should you use instead? Here are some alternatives listed in order of the ones I like best!

1. **Vance's Dairy Free** – Creamy, mild, pleasant flavored non-dairy powder milk made from potatoes. Rich in calcium and vitamins, low in sugar. Since it is in a powder form, it makes it easy to travel. The best way to make it is a pitcher with an aeration plunger. Measure out the milk, mix with about 1-2 cups of hot water to dissolve the powder quickly and easily, then add the cold water and aerate again to mix well. It keeps up to a week in the refrigerator. They also make a dairy free chocolate version.

2. **Soy Milk** – There are many types of soy milk available at your grocery store. When my daughter first started, we had to purchase it at a health food store, now, most major food chains stock a variety of brands. You can purchase refrigerated soy milk in the dairy case – from original to vanilla, from chocolate to strawberry. Test which one your child likes best.

You can also purchase Soy milk in the health food area as well. These containers are sealed and do not need to be refrigerated until they are opened. This makes it easy to stock up or to travel.

NOTE: Some children may self-addict to soy products. If you notice that they can't seem to get enough soy milk in a day, you may have to eliminate and then reintroduce a cup a day at a time.

Watch your child's behavior during this time and see if you notice any differences.

3. **Rice Milk** – You must be very careful in choosing this type of substitute. **Some of them carry trace amounts of barley which contain gluten.** Read all labels carefully. These also come in juice box form and can be a great carry along drink.

4. **Almond Milk** – Another flavorful alternative to regular milk. Made in various flavors, and as long as your child has no allergies to nuts, this is a terrific alternative which other family members may enjoy as well

In addition to milk, you must take out the following:

1. **Yogurt** – There are tasty alternatives in your grocer's dairy section – as the general population is more dairy sensitive, new products come out every day.

2. **Cheese** – Unfortunately, in my opinion, there are no good casein free cheese that tastes good. On one occasion, my half-sister who is also a vegetarian, told me about this great soy cheese. She brought it to a party to have my daughter taste it. When I saw the way it melted, I was convinced it had casein in it (this is the dairy protein). She was sure since it said VEGAN that it was safe, but when she got home and checked the label, it did contain casein.

My general rule is that if the cheese melts like cheese, it has casein in it. If it doesn't melt, it's probably okay, but will not have much flavor. We have chosen to just eliminate it.

3. **Butter** - Look for soy spreads, Spectrum Brand Spread, or Fleischman's unsalted. Just make sure that there are no butter solids, whey (a dairy by-product), or casein.

4. **Ice Cream/Non-Dairy Treats** – Freeze Pops are a good choice during summer – although loaded with sugar and food coloring. These treats are handy to have in the freezer for when the kids are playing outside on a hot day. Soy Ice Cream is available in vanilla, chocolate and strawberry, and is so good; I bet most of you couldn't

tell the difference if I served it for dessert. There are also wonderful selections of gluten free ice cream cones.

BEWARE OF SHERBET – many a family member will try and convince you that sherbet is not ice cream, but it contains milk solids.

Sometimes it seems that the child with the special diet ruins the summer favorite of going out for ice cream for the rest of the family. If you are headed out to the Dairy Queen®, your GF/CF child can order a dairy free Star. At Culvers® they can get the summer favorite, Lemon Ice and at Cold Stone Creamery®, and other such ice cream shops they often have a dairy free sorbet.

After eliminating dairy, you should notice some behavior changes in your child. Maybe they will not rock as much, or maybe they will begin to be more alert, and offer more eye contact. In my daughter's case, we noticed that she didn't flap her hands any more. Keep a log or diary if you must to help document the changes that you observe.

Bread…. Gluten's Biggest Friend

Bread is probably the trickiest of all things to eliminate. There are many types of bread on the market: rice, soy, quinoa, bean, or a mix of different flours. Some of them taste like stale paper; others are only good if you microwave the slice for 30 seconds. The family favorite is the Rice Sandwich bread made by Kinickinick Foods. This is the closest to the real thing you can find without making it yourself. But even this bread must be kept frozen and is much better when microwaved for a few seconds to increase the moisture and texture.

Loaves of bread are expensive – some averaging as much as $6.00 a loaf. There are mixes available to help you cut corners and make a homemade loaf. Although you can make them in a bread machine, I recommend mixing the recipe in a bowl and baking the mix in the oven.

Slice the bread with an electric knife to get even thinner slices and freeze immediately.

If you have time to try homemade, see my recipe in the back of the book.

> **Helpful Hint:** Whether you bake the bread yourself or buy it ready-made, before freezing, separate the slices so that they can be removed slice by slice when frozen. Or, invest in small freezer bags and individually freeze one or two slices to have them handy to make sandwiches.

Snacks

Snacks are relatively simple. There are many ready to purchase snacks that are okay. Tortilla chips, potato chips, and corn chips are okay, just watch for the flavored chips or chips in the cans, such as Pringles® as they often contain wheat flour. Whenever possible try and stay away from hydrogenated oils. These are not good for anyone, but the fewer processed ingredients the better.

Pretzels were the one thing off the list! But now, there are many brands that are sold right in the snack aisle of the regular grocery store.

Crackers – This used to be a hard staple to replace, but today there are so many choices, just always check the ingredients.

Puddings and Gelatin – Although there are some warnings of food colorings, etc. in gelatin, I find this overall to be a good treat. Again, if you find your child obsesses about this snack, it probably isn't good for them, but once or twice a week as a lunch snack is probably okay.

Pudding is obviously a no-no due to the milk, but there are some mixes available by Imagine® that you can make with soy milk or Dairy Free®. To the regular palette, they are okay, but to those used to a GF/CF diet, they can be a nice treat.

Breakfast

Thanks to the health-consciousness of the population, GF/CF food is easier to come by and there are lots of good cereals that kids love. Some of our favorites are Barbara's Organic Brown Rice Crisps®, Enviro Kidz brand including a Koala Crisp®, Gorilla Munch®, Frosted Flakes and Panda Puffs®. Cheerios® and Chex® has become gluten free and so have many other cereals - check the ingredients and always look for the hidden gluten.

Waffles and pancakes are a great breakfast. There are good frozen waffles and almost every store now carries a variety of ready-to-make mixes – just add eggs and water to make delicious pancakes and waffles. If you do not have the mix on hand, try my recipe to whip up your own homemade pancakes and waffles – make extra and freeze for use during the week. I even pre-package my own dry ingredients. Then during the week when I am pressed for time, I can quickly add eggs and dairy free milk and whip up some fresh pancakes!

Syrup of choice should be the real thing – pure maple syrup has no additives and a great taste. Use sparingly as it has a high sugar content.

Helpful Hint: Both frozen waffles and pancakes taste better if you defrost them in the microwave instead of toasting them. They are moister and taste more like the real deal.

Lunches

If your child is off to school, the school cafeteria will offer them nothing – most lunch menus are loaded with wheat, dairy and high fat/fried foods. The best bet it to get your child used to eating homemade sandwiches and maybe some soup. The favorite at our house is the classic PBJ (peanut butter and jelly). We use real peanut butter and squeezable jellies (so the rest of the family doesn't double dip the knife!). Small bags or chips or pretzels, a piece of fruit or carrots always make a well balanced lunch. If your child yearns for a Lunchable®, make your own! Ideas and recipes are in the back. A GF/CF cookie is always a special treat – For some tasty ideas see the dessert section!

Dinner

Believe it or not, most of what you probably make for dinner can be modified to be GF/CF or may actually be GF/CF without trying! Obviously fried chicken and mashed potatoes are out, but baked chicken and baked potatoes are just fine.

Rice is a staple in my family, and grilling a steak or making a pot roast adds no gluten (if you use flour as a thickener in your own recipes use corn starch instead).

I have included dinner ideas and recipes to help you feed your entire family without making two meals.

Pasta

There are many varieties of pasta that are wheat free. They are made in different shapes from macaroni style to lasagna. Corn pasta and quinoa pastas are firmer and less soggy than some of the rice or potato pastas. Experiment and see which one your child likes.

Helpful Hint! Be careful not to overcook the pasta – it gets soggy. Add a drop of olive oil to the boiling water to help prevent sticking.

Again, cheese or any type of Parmesan topping is usually prohibited. There are soy versions but most of them contain casein. Check the labels.

If you would like to top it off with sauce, remember to check the label. I would avoid sauces with high fructose corn syrup as these can cause hyper-activity. Stick to organic marinara sauces and make sure there are no added cheese products or whey.

Saturday Night Pizza

Let's face it – everyone loves pizza. Unfortunately, from the hand tossed wheat crust to the gooey mozzarella topping, regular pizza is not a reality on a GF/CF diet. But do not dismay – there are ways to get around this. If you are starting your child on the diet at a young age, the GF/CF way will be how they think pizza should be! If you are trying to start this with an older child, one who already loves the cheesy, crispy, stuffed crust version, this will be a little more challenging.

You can make your own pizza crust, see recipe section, or go the cheater way – Kinickinick foods makes the most awesome personal pan size crusts. They come 4 to a package and they make pizza making easy! There are also other brands in the freezer section of your regular grocery store. You may have to try several brands to get the one that tastes the best for your pallet, but it will be worth it.

Although I do not use any cheese on my pizza, I use a wonderful, flavorful organic pizza sauce made by Muir Glen. It is distributed by Small Planet Foods and I have found the brand at most major food chains. I layer on a nice amount of this sauce on the crust and bake in a toaster oven or regular oven until just slightly brown. Add your child's favorite vegetables and even pepperoni or crumbled Italian sausage.

Helpful Hint: Pizza can be a fun thing for you and your child. Let him/her help prepare the pizza, and ask if they would like to try sautéed mushrooms or green peppers! Let him/her be creative!

And…thanks to all those who are now taking gluten out of their diet, you can order pizza from many local pizza places (especially in Chicago). I order my daughter's pizza with sausage, but no cheese. They are really good and make family pizza night fun again!

Desserts

In my opinion, no life is complete without dessert. Although in my interaction with many parents who are doing the diet with their children, many just have their kids forgo dessert; I believe that dessert is not only just a favorite food, but a social component as well. Let's face it – how many times do you get together with friends for cake and coffee. Or at a kid's birthday party – will yours be the only one without dessert?

I always tried to help my daughter feel "normal" among her peers, so when she was young both her class teacher and her daycare provider had an emergency stash of special snacks.

Although she knows she can't have the cream filled chocolate frosted cupcake little Suzy brought in for her birthday, she knows that she can go to her special treat bag and pick something out.

I love to bake, so making special cakes, donuts, cookies and cupcakes are never a problem. Manufacturers seem to be aware of many of the food allergies and are now labeling their food and even taking gluten and casein out of their foods along with trans-fats and other unhealthy additives, making it easier to find pre-prepared foods that are good tasting.

Plus, many daycares need to have pre-packaged unopened foods to comply with the health department and so this can be easily accomplished.

Baking

If you are a baker at heart – you should really enjoy the challenge of baking gluten/casein free. I love to bake and find it rewarding when I can come up with a cookie, cake, or bread recipe that my daughter gobbles up and her friends can enjoy without knowing it is GF/CF. Vicky has even started formulating her own cupcake recipes and they are added in the dessert section.

If you plan to be a GF/CF baker – the following items are a must have in your kitchen:

- A good Mix Master (I recommend a Kitchen Aide Stand Mixer)
- Muffin Pans, Cookie Sheets, Bundt Pans
- Donut Pan (or a really fun contraption that makes donuts like waffles)
- Measuring cups/spoons
- Parchment paper
- Non Stick Spray

These should only be used to make GF/CF items. This eliminated the possibility of cross contamination from making food for the rest of your family.

Flour

You must always have an ample supply of GF/CF flour on hand. I make it by the container full and here is a quick way of mixing the necessary flours.

- 5 lbs. White Rice Flour
- 2 lbs. of Potato Starch
- 1 lbs. of Tapioca Flour

Mix the above flours in an airtight container – the flour will be ready when you are!

> **Note:** There are other GF/CF flours available on the market. You can choose soy flour, bean flours (which add protein), sweet rice flour, brown rice flour.

Xantham Gum or Guar Gum

This is a necessary ingredient in GF/CF baking. This is what replaces the gluten to give baked goods their dough like texture – if you forget to add it, your items will crumble.

Add one tablespoon per cup of GF/CF flour mix above.

Baking Powder and Vanilla

These are two necessary ingredients for baking that surprised me with a gluten factor!

Baking powder may contain wheat flour and an anti-caking agent and vanilla may be extracted with a wheat-based alcohol. Check the labels to see if they say they are gluten free.

Semi-Sweet Chocolate Chips!

Chocolate Chip cookies are a basic childhood necessity! In the back of this book are two recipes that make a large batch of cookies so you are not always baking.

Look for dairy free chocolate chips. The chips also make great little chocolate snacks. When other kids are eating M&M's, your little one can have a chocolate treat too! I also melt them and use candy forms to make suckers and candy shapes.

Helpful Hint! The chocolate chip cookie recipes at the end of this book make a lot of cookies. If you do not need the whole batch, or just do not have time to bake them all, roll them into small balls and freeze them. When you need more cookies, it is just as convenient as the store pre-made cookie dough that is ready to bake!

WHAT ELSE CAN I FEED MY CHILD?

There are many helpful websites that can help you navigate this diet. See the appendix at the end of the book.

What else do I do in my family? I cook gluten free in most of my recipes. Meat loaf? I use corn meal or gluten free bread crumbs. Soups? I purchase GF soup base and use fresh chicken.

Hamburger, Oscar Meyer Ham, and just plain old chicken are the favorite meats in my house. White Rice is always a great side dish. (Purchase a rice cooker and it always tastes like your favorite Chinese restaurant). There are many marinades and salad dressings that are GF, or you can make your own! See the recipes section for details.

Fresh and frozen produce are a must for any well balanced diet. Freeze green grapes and they are just like candy!

Apples and Apple Juice, Bananas, and Red Grapes

I suggest you remove apples and apple juice from your child's diet immediately.

My daughter would eat apples by the bag and drink juice by the gallons. I thought it was healthy!

Well, it turns out that she is highly sensitive to the phenol sulfates that naturally occur in the fruits. Her behavior changed radically the minute she consumed any apples or juice – even juice blends with apples as an ingredient.

Instead, we use Asian pears, red pears and Bartlett pears. She enjoys peaches and melon as well. Orange juice and white grape juice are good juice substitutes for apple juice. Water can serve just as well – shouldn't we all have more water anyway?

In conclusion......

Well, there may never be a finish line for you or your child...but it does get easier. Teach your child how to eat, tell him/her that the reason you are taking away foods in because he/she may feel sick when they eat certain foods. After your child has been off the foods for a while, when GF/CF ingredients are accidentally ingested your child probably will not feel well. He/she may get stomach cramps or diarrhea, or just feel more edgy.

A LITTLE ABOUT
BIOMEDICAL RESEARCH

The diet does not do it all. You need a comprehensive plan to suit your child's needs. My belief is that the diet opened pathways to my daughter's brain making it possible for her to learn easier. She seemed to respond better to all her therapies and many of her sensitivities and autistic behaviors have subsided since the diet. I want to stress however, that we worked closely with a doctor who provides care on the "biomedical" side of the equation.

We provided our daughter daily with supplements like DMG, 5HTP, Methyl B^{12}, Calcium, Zinc, L-Glutathione and selenium when she was younger. We also use homeopathic treatments to help her levels of heavy metals and levels of immunity from vaccines.

My recommendation is that you look to see if there is a doctor in your area who provides services for these alternative approaches. Many regular physicians do not believe that the diet works. I was actually at an autism conference where a doctor was going over all the pharmaceutical drug therapies that are available. When I asked about the diet, he immediately put me down, told me there were no medical studies proving the diet has any impact, but it if made me "feel better" it would not do any harm to my child.

Believe me, this is not an easy task. I never did this to make myself "feel better". Ask any parent who has seen the change in their child, even if it is only slight; those parents will tell you that it is worth it.

You will probably come across many nay-sayers while pursuing this type of treatment. Watch your child and persevere. For many children on the spectrum the diet, the supplements and alternative therapies may not have an effect – but for many they do and it is certainly worth trying. I watched my little girl play with friends, do her school work and work hard at living in the "normal" world. It was exhausting on some days and rewarding on most. There was a time when I couldn't leave the house without a tantrum looming in the distance. If the activity was not on the picture schedule, it was not going to happen that day. Today, she lives in an apartment with two friends and is going to college, driving, and working part-time. Life found its way and I am grateful for help of therapists, teachers, support groups, family, and faith.

If you ever have any questions or want to vent – you can contact me anytime – the road you walk may seem empty, but in truth, you walk with a crowd...let's help each other.

PART IV

Recipes

TABLE OF CONTENTS FOR RECIPES

BREAKFAST

LUNCH IDEAS

DINNER IDEAS

MARINADES AND SALAD DRESSINGS

DESSERTS

BREADS AND ROLLS

BREAKFAST

WAFFLES

2 Cups GF Flour Mix
2 TBSP. of Xantham or Guar Gum
1 TBSP. of sugar
4 tsp. of GF Baking Powder
½ tsp. Salt

2 eggs
½ cup canola oil
1 ¾ cup of milk substitute*

Heat waffle iron
Mix together dry ingredients.
Beat eggs with hand beater or fork until fluffy.
Add eggs and oil to dry ingredients – mix.
Add milk substitute until batter is smooth.

Pour batter from cup or pitcher onto center of hot waffle iron. Bake about 3-4 minutes. Remove waffle carefully.

Makes about 10 square waffles – let cool before freezing

PANCAKES

2 Cups GF Flour Mix
2 TBSP. of Xantham or Guar Gum
3 tsp. of GF Baking Powder
½ tsp. of Salt
1 TBSP. of Sugar

1 egg
2 TBSP. of Canola Oil
1 Cup of milk substitute*

*add more or less to get batter to good consistency. Soy milk is thicker, so you may need to add a little water.

Mix together dry ingredients
Beat egg with fork or hand whip until fluffy.
Add to dry ingredients, add milk until smooth (you may need to add a little more milk to get right consistency – it depends on what type of milk substitute you are using.)

Spray griddle or frying pan with non-stick canola oil – pour about 1/3 cup batter for each pancake. Cook pancakes until bubbly in the middle, then turn. Make 12 pancakes.

You can add fresh blueberries to make blueberry pancakes.
Add dairy free chocolate chips to make fun chocolate chip pancakes!

SCRAMBLED EGGS

Mix 2 eggs until frothy.

Melt a pat of dairy free margarine (Spectrum or Fleischman's Unsalted) in a small frying pan – add eggs.

As egg mixture begins to set lift the cooked portions and let the uncooked portions flow into the pan. Cook until eggs are thick but still moist.

Salt and pepper to taste.
You can add bacon (Oscar Meyer center cut is the best) or ham (Oscar Meyer has no wheat fillers) to the eggs to make heartier scrambled eggs.

BLUEBERRY MUFFINS

Preheat oven to 400°F

2 Cups GF Flour Mix
2 TBSP. of Xantham or Guar Gum
3 tsp. of GF Baking Powder
1 tsp. Salt

¾ Cup Milk Substitute
½ Cup Canola Oil
1 egg

1 Cup of Fresh Blueberries

Sift dry ingredients together.
Mix together wet ingredients.

Add eggs, milk and oil mixture to flour mix and stir well, adding a little more milk substitute as needed.

Fold in blueberries.

Divide mixture among muffin cups and sprinkle with a little sugar. Bake until golden brown, 18 to 20 minutes in a 400°F oven.

LUNCH IDEAS

When you have young children in school, packing a lunch can be challenging. Most children with autism have lots of texture problems so fortunately, if you find something your child likes to eat for lunch, he/she may not have a problem eating the same lunch every day.

"UNCRUSTABLE" PBJ'S

You have all seen the newest addition to the packaged take along lunch! These round, crustless peanut butter and jelly sandwiches are pre-packaged so you can just throw them in the lunch box. They are every mom's dream.

Okay, so those with kids on the diet do not get to have it quite so convenient, but it is still possible to get that round, gooey jelly filled circle sandwich gluten free!

> 2 slices of GF bread from the freezer, defrosted for two minutes, then microwave for 20 seconds.

> Spread on your favorite gluten free peanut butter or your favorite almond butter and jelly of choice.

Although we have eliminated purple or red grapes from my daughter's diet, I have found that the teaspoon or so of Welches squeezable grape jelly had no effect on her behavior – so you may want to experiment.

Then, to make that perfectly round sealed sandwich I used a special tool which I purchased from the Pampered Chef® called the "Cut n Seal." It sells for about $10.00 and is a fun way to make crustless sandwiches.

Add some GF potato chips, little carrots, or some green grapes, and you have a healthy, easy lunch and your child's lunch will not look much different than the other kids!

HOMEMADE LUNCHABLES®

Another lunch time phenomenon was the Oscar Meyer™ Lunchable! These cute prepacked lunches with little circles of ham, cheese, crackers, juice box and a special treat are many a parents' survival of that quick lunch that you do not have to pack.

Again, for parents of kids on the diet, the convenience of these types of food is lost to us, but often time our kids want to feel special and have this unique lunch. With a little time and effort your special diet child can have his or her own Lunchable!

- Buy a container with special smaller dividers in it or buy a Lunchable – (you eat the contents) and save the container!

- Take your child's favorite ham or turkey and cut the slices into circles with a small cookie or biscuit cutter.

- Forget the cheese since there is no good substitute.

- Then take GF crackers or the small wheat free rice thins and put a stack of those in the container.

- Take a lemonade, orange juice box, or other favorite pouch drink

- Add a cookie or a special dairy free chocolate.

Imagine the delight when your child opens his/her lunch to find their very own Lunchable! I am sure he/she will be the envy of the other kids at the table.

SANDWICHES

If your child doesn't get hung up on the fancy uncrustable sandwiches or Lunchables, a good old fashioned sandwich may be just the ticket.

Choose lunch meats that are free from wheat fillers and add mayo or mustard to their tastes.

HOT DOGS

Another lunch favorite is the hot dog. Oscar Meyer or Vienna All Beef Hot Dogs (watch ingredients closely) are a staple in my fridge. If you go out, most hot dog stands (especially in Chicago) have the Vienna All beef and we just order it without the bun. Some places even offer gluten free buns. Look for your favorite GF hot dog buns, add your child's favorite condiments and enjoy.

HAMBURGERS

There is no change to this all American lunch or dinner – When going out, just order the hamburger without the bun or order a GF bun available at many restaurants these days. At home a juicy grilled burger is always a summer treat. Kinnikinnick™ has great GFCF Hamburger buns that creates a wonderful treat. There are also many other brands in your local grocery store. Load it up with GF ketchup or some lettuce and tomatoes and your child has a tasty treat.

Note: Watch out for boxed hamburgers that are already seasoned – they often have flavoring that contain wheat or wheat fillers – best to stick with 100% ground beef.

HOMEMADE FRENCH FRIES

Just peel a potato, cut up into fry shapes and deep fry in canola oil! If you do not have a deep fryer just take a small frying pan and heat up some canola oil. Once hot, place a shallow layer of fries into the pan and cook until golden brown.

A note on restaurant French Fries. In the early stages, you must avoid cross contamination as much as possible. Restaurants often fry other, wheat coated foods in the oil they cook their fries in. Ask the restaurant if they use the oil for any other foods. Once your child has been on the diet for a while, he/she may not be sensitive to small amounts – you just have to watch behavior. I have always found McDonald's® French fries were okay.

CHICKEN SALAD

This one will definitely be an acquired taste – definitely for the older, less tactile taste bud – but even those on a non GF/CF diet will love this salad.

> 4 Boneless Chicken Breasts
> Salt/Pepper to taste
> Splash of Olive Oil
>
> 1 green onion
> 10 green grapes
> 1 TBSP. of mayonnaise (more or less to taste)
> salt and pepper to taste.

Put chicken in baking dish season with salt and pepper. Drizzle with olive oil and bake at 350° about 25 minutes until chicken juices run clear.

When cool, cut chicken into cubes.

Take a tablespoon of finely chopped onions, green grapes cut in half and a little mayonnaise. Mix together using more or less mayo to taste. Stuff in a tomato or just eat plain with a few GF crackers and you have a nice light lunch.

Hint: When you make the chicken breasts, bake a few, chunk and freeze. Defrost and you are you ready to make your salad.

DINNER IDEAS

This is when the GF/CF diet can either be the hardest or easiest! Many of the foods you already make are GF/CF, but if you have a picky eater, you will find yourself making two meals each night. Parties can be especially hard. In this section, I have tried to give you a variety of recipes that you can make for the whole family and that your GF/CF child will enjoy as well.

As every child is different, tactile senses to different meats may be a problem. For instance, my daughter used to not like any kind of red meat unless it was ground. Although my pepper steak melts like butter, she did not like the texture of this meat. Now, she breaks the bank at a restaurant savoring prime rib or crab legs! You will have to try out the different recipes to see what your child likes best – and you can always make a double batch and freeze individual portions so on the night the rest of you are not eating GF/CF, you can just defrost and heat a single serving of a favorite food.

STUFFED PEPPERS

(Makes about 4 peppers)

> 1 lb. ground beef
> 1 cup rice (not instant)
> ¼ cup finely chopped onion
> Salt/pepper to taste
> 4 small green peppers with tops cut off and seeded.
> 1 large can tomatoes – stewed or whole

Mix ground beef, rice, onion, salt and pepper in a bowl.

Make 4 balls of meat and "stuff" into cut open peppers.

Place in pressure cooker. Pour tomatoes over stuffed peppers and seal lid of cooker. Add water to cover ingredients in pot.

After pressure cooker weight begins to jiggle- use 10 lbs. of pressure - cook about 15 minutes.

You can make this in the oven as well, although they may not be as moist. Place in covered casserole and bake at 350° for about 40 minutes.

"GARBAGE" – PEPPER STEAK

When I was little, my mom used to make this recipe all the time. It got its name because she often used leftover vegetables and tougher cuts of meat. When we asked her what she was making, she would answer "Garbage"! However, it is also known as a version of Pepper Steak!

> 1-2 lbs. of round steak cut into small pieces
> 1 medium onion, wedged
> 7 - 3" pieces of celery
> 1 green pepper, seeded and cut into chunks
> 1 whole tomato, chunked
> 1 tsp. allspice (whole or ground)
> 1 tsp. oregano

In a pressure cooker, brown meat in a little olive oil on both sides, sprinkle with salt and pepper. Add other ingredients, sprinkling oregano over the top. Add water to cover.

Cook 30 minutes after weight begins to jiggle. Use 10 lbs. of pressure.

ALTERNATE METHOD:

You prepare the meal the same way, but instead of placing in a pressure cooker, put in a slow cooker and cook on high for 2-3 hours or low for 4-6 hours.

MEATLOAF

A family favorite especially if you are on a budget.

> 2 lbs. ground meat
> 1 lb. ground pork
> 1 small onion diced
> ½ cup GF/CF Bread crumbs, corn meal, or GF oatmeal
> Salt/pepper to taste

Mix all ingredients together and form a loaf.
Place in a loaf pan and cover with a small can of tomato sauce.

Bake at 350° for 30 minutes.
You can also put this in a slow cooker on low for 6 hours or high for 3 hours with a little water in the bottom of the pan.

SEASONED CHICKEN

Baked chicken is always a favorite in my house. Whether it is boneless or bone in chicken, baking a cut up chicken seasoned with your favorite spices is always a sure bet.

WHOLE CHICKEN

1 whole chicken, rinsed and brined in salt water for about ½ hour.
Rub with olive oil and then season with salt, pepper, and poultry spices.
Place in shallow roasting pan or casserole dish.
Add about 1 cup of water to the bottom of the pan
Cover and bake at 350°F for an hour
Add celery and carrots and onion slices around the chicken to add extra flavor before baking.

GF STUFFING MIX:

For a small baking chicken, toast 10 pieces of GF Bread and cube.

> 2-3 stalks of celery - diced
> 1 small onion – chopped
> 1 Tsp. Thyme
> salt and pepper to taste
> 1 cup GF chicken broth

Melt 1-2 tsp. of CF butter in an open skillet. Sautee celery and onion until onion is clear.
Add sautéed onion/celery to cubed bread.
Add Thyme, salt and pepper and GF chicken broth

Stuff in cavity of chicken.
Baking time may increase by 10-15 minutes due to stuffing – make sure internal temperature is 165°F.

BAKED CHICKEN PIECES

For cut up chicken, rub a little olive oil into the skin of each piece and salt and pepper to taste.
Arrange in baking dish.

Add other favorite spices – Italian or spicy.

You can also brush with a little GF/CF BBQ sauce (see appendix for brands).
Add green peppers, onions, celery or carrots

Bake at 350ºF for 30-45 minutes until juices run clear.

CHINESE CHICKEN

A quick, easy recipe!

> 4 boneless chicken breasts-cubed
> 1 small onion, chopped
> 2 stalks celery chopped
> 1 cup frozen green beans
> 1 can water chestnuts
> 1 can bean sprouts or 1 cup of fresh bean sprouts
> 1/3 cup wheat free Tamari sauce
> 4 TBSP of canola oil
> 1 cup GF Chicken Broth

In a large frying pan or wok, heat 3 TBSP of oil
Cook chicken until no longer pink
Remove chicken pieces
Add onion, celery, green beans another TBSP of canola oil
Stir fry until onions are clear
Add chicken back to mixture
Add water chestnuts and bean sprouts
Add Tamari sauce and let simmer for 15 minutes
Add 1 tsp. of corn starch to ¼ cup of cold water and stir in mixture to thicken sauce

Serve over rice.

BBQ PULLED PORK, BEEF, CHICKEN

2-3 lb. pork roast or
2-3 lb. roast beef
4-5 boneless chicken breasts.

3-4 cups of water
1 TBSP. of garlic salt
1 TBSP. dried onion flakes
1 tsp. sugar
1 TBSP. of oregano
1 TBSP. basil
1 TBSP. parsley
2 TBSP. pepper
¼ cup apple cider vinegar

Choose one of the meats above and put into slow cooker with water and spices. Cook on low for 4-6 hours.

When meat easily shreds, pull apart and add juice to meat to keep a good moist consistency.

Add apple cider vinegar and BBQ sauce and serve on GF buns.

PORK ROAST WITH PEARS

Pork roast or pork tenderloin
salt/pepper
½ tsp. rosemary
2 pears, peeled and halved

Rinse pork and pat with salt and pepper.
Place in baking dish and sprinkle with Rosemary.
Place pears around the roast – add about 1 cup of water to bottom of pan.
Bake at 350°F degrees until meat thermometer reads 170°F.

Slice and serve with a tossed salad and rice.

GRILLED TILAPIA OR SALMON

4-6 pieces of Tilapia or Salmon steaks.

Prepare a foil packet by laying out a 4x4 sheet of foil, spray it with non-stick vegetable spray and lay the fish pieces in each foil square.

Drizzle with olive oil and add spice of your choice – cumin for spice, fresh basil and oregano for savory flavor and salt and pepper, garlic powder, or any other spice that is GF.

Place a slice of lemon in each packet.
Seal each packet and grill for about 10-15 minutes or until fish flakes and separate easily.

You can also place in oven at 350ºF for 20-25 minutes or until fish is flaky.

PASTA

1 cup cooked, any type of GF pasta

1 cup red sauce (Look for canned sauces that do not contain any cheeses or flour thickeners. Marinara is usually the best)

2-3 Italian sausage links – grilled or broiled in oven or removed from skin and browned in frying pan.

Cook pasta and drain.

Mix with favorite pasta sauce and pour over pasta.

GF MEATBALLS

1 lb. ground beef
1/4 cup corn meal or GF bread crumbs
1 egg
Salt and Pepper to taste

Mix together all of the above. Make into round meatballs, any size. Place on baking sheet lined with parchment paper.
Bake at 400° for 20 minutes.
Serve with pasta or just red sauce on a GF hotdog bun for a meatball sandwich.

HOMEMADE CHICKEN SOUP

2 boneless/skinless or bone-in with skin chicken breasts
3 stalks celery
1 onion quartered 8 cups of water
4 tsp. or 4 cubes GF chicken base
1 tsp. allspice
1 tsp. basil
1 tsp. oregano
1 tsp. sea salt

Place all ingredients into large soup pot and simmer for 30-40 minutes until chicken is done.

Remove chicken pieces and dice into small pieces. Strain soup of all veggies and spices. Add chicken and additional salt and pepper to taste. Serve with GF noodles or white rice.

This soup freezes great – so double the recipe and you will always have soup ready!

*Note: using bone-in with skin chicken will make the soup more flavorful.

RED HOT CHILI

2 – 16 oz. cans of dark red kidney beans (drained)
2 – 14 oz. cans of diced or crushed tomatoes
2 lbs. ground meat, browned and drained (you can use ground turkey or beef)
2 medium onions chopped
1 green pepper chopped
2 cloves of garlic, crushed
2-3 TBLS. of chili powder
1 tsp. of cumin
Salt and pepper to taste.

Put all ingredients in crock pot. Stir. Cook low 10-12 hours, or high 5-6 hours.

You may also cook on the stovetop – 2-3 hours - medium heat – add water as needed.

SPANISH RICE

1 cup of long grain rice
1/2 cup of canola oil
1 small onion – diced
1 clove of garlic or pinch of garlic powder
2 cups of water
1 cube or 1 tsp. of GF chicken base
1 small can of tomato sauce

Rinse rice in warm water and soak for 10 minutes
In sauce pan, heat the oil and add the drained rice
Fry the rice, onion, and garlic together for about 5 minutes
Drain the oil
Add tomato sauce, water, chicken base, and salt to taste
Cover and let simmer until the rice absorbs all the water. (about 15-18 minutes)
Be careful not to burn the rice
Serve as a side dish to your favorite meal

Helpful Hint: This rice can be tricky – you need to make sure you soak it, and do not fry it too hard, or your rice can be soggy or crunchy. If you accidentally burn the rice, take a damp paper towel and place it over the rice. Cover and let sit for about 5 minutes. The towel absorbs the burnt taste. It works well on plain white rice as well.

TACOS

1 lb. ground beef browned, or
3 boneless chicken breasts baked and shredded
or strips of flank steak seasoned with salt and pepper,
grilled or broiled
1 can of diced tomatoes with hot Chile peppers
Salt and Pepper to taste

Mix browned ground beef or shredded chicken or strips of flank steak with tomatoes and salt and pepper in a frying pan.
Stir until all ingredients are mixed and warmed through.
Serve on hard corn taco shells or soft corn tortillas that have been warmed in the microwave for 35 -50 seconds.
Add lettuce and salsa to add more flavor.

MARINADES AND SALAD DRESSINGS

There are many over the counter brands that are safe to use as marinades and salad dressings. Check out the web sites that offer GF/CF products and choose from their wide offerings. If you are in a pinch and need to make a quick Italian style dressing or marinade, here is one that you can always whip up in a jiffy.

ITALIAN MARINADE/DRESSING

1 cup canola oil
1/4 cup rice vinegar
2 Tbsp. of chopped onion
1 tsp. sugar
1 tsp. dried basil leaves
1 tsp. dried oregano
1/4 tsp. black pepper
1 clove garlic, crushed
1/4 tsp. crushed red pepper

Mix all ingredients in a covered container, pour over meat and refrigerate 2-4 hours. Great for grilled marinated chicken, pork chops or steaks. Refrigerate leftovers and use for salads.

BBQ SAUCE

1 cup GF/CF ketchup
1/2 small onion, chopped finely
1/3 cup water
1/4 cup of CF margarine
1 Tbsp. Paprika
1 tsp. brown sugar
1/2 tsp. salt
1/4 tsp. pepper
1/4 cup lemon juice
1 Tbsp. Tamari sauce

Heat all ingredients expect lemon juice and Tamari sauce, until boiling. Stir in lemon juice and Tamari sauce. Makes about 2 cups.

DESSERTS

CHOCOLATE CHIP COOKIES (#1)

1 cup canola oil
1 cup CF margarine (softened)
2 eggs
1 cup sugar
1 cup brown sugar
2 tsp. GF Vanilla
1 tsp. Baking Soda
1/2 tsp. salt
4 cups GF Flour Mix 4 tsp.
4 tsp. Xantham Gum
1 bag CF chocolate chips

In mixmaster bowl, beat oil, margarine and sugar until fluffy. Add eggs and vanilla. Sift dry ingredients together and add to wet mixture slowly. Blend well (I recommend high for 2-3 minutes). Stir in chocolate chips.

Drop dough on baking sheet lined with parchment paper by rounded tablespoons. Press down with fingers to flatten cookies. Bake at 350 for 10-12 minutes. Place on cookie rack to cool.

Makes about 4 dozen cookies

Note: GF/CF cookies are a little more fragile until cooled. Store in plastic container with lid – you may also freeze (up to 3 months).

CHOCOLATE CHIP COOKIES (#2)

(These are more cake-like cookies)

> 1 lb. CF margarine, softened
> 6 eggs slightly beaten
> 1 cup sugar
> 1 cup brown sugar
> 2 tsp. GF vanilla
> 2 tsp. baking soda
> 2 tsp. baking powder
> 1 tsp. salt
> 5 cups GF flour mix
> 5 tsp. xantham Gum
> 1 bag CF chocolate chips

In mix master bowl, beat margarine and sugar until fluffy. Add eggs and vanilla. Sift dry ingredients and blend well (I recommend high for 2-3 minutes). Stir in chocolate chips.

Drop dough on baking sheet lined with parchment paper by rounded teaspoons. Bake at 375°F for 8-10 minutes.

Makes about 7 dozen cookies

Remember you can drop dough on foil, wax paper or parchment paper and freeze. Bake when you need them! Just make sure you store them in an airtight container (up to 3-4 months).

You can also bake them and then freeze in freezer storage bag.

PEANUT BUTTER COOKIES

2 eggs
2 cups peanut butter
2 cups sugar

Mix together all ingredients. Shape into balls the size of walnuts and place on cookie sheet lined with parchment paper. Bake in preheated 375ºF oven for 10 minutes. Take a fork dipped in sugar and press a crisscross pattern into each cookie. Bake for 1 minute more.

Remove from pan, cool.

To add a chocolate treat, instead of crisscrossing cookies with fork, press in 3 dairy free chocolate chips and bake for 1 more minute.

Makes about 5 dozen cookies.

SPRITZ COOKIES

1 cup CF margarine, softened
1/2 cup sugar
2 ¼ cups of GF Flour Mix, sifted
2 tsp. Xantham Gum
1/2 tsp. salt
1 egg
1 tsp. GF Vanilla Extract

Heat oven to 400°F.

Cream together margarine and sugar. Add remaining ingredients. Beat for about 2 minutes.

Place dough in cookie press, and put cookies on parchment lined cookie sheet. Bake for 6-9 minutes – watch so they do not get too brown.

For fancy decorated cookies, sprinkle with colored sugar. You can purchase raw sugar and tint with food coloring to make your own!

Immediately remove to cooling rack. Makes about 5 dozen.

CRISP RICE TREATS

30 Large GF marshmallows (recommend Kraft Jet Puffed®)
1/4 cup of CF margarine
1/2 tsp GF vanilla
5 cups GF crisp rice cereal

Heat marshmallows and margarine in large saucepan on low heat until smooth.

Add vanilla and cereal until well coated. Press into a 9x9 pan which has been sprayed with canola oil. Let cool, cut into bars, about 2x1. Yields about 36 bars.

S'MORES

Roast 1 GF/CF large marshmallow until done. Place on 1/2 GF cracker. Sprinkle on a few CF chocolate chips. Place other half of GF cracker and press together!

CAKES WITH FROSTING

To make an easy birthday cake, my favorite cake mix is made by the Really Great Food Company®. It is a box cake that can be made into two loaf cakes, 4 8x8 cakes, 1 Bundt pan, or two 9" layer cakes.

It freezes wonderfully, so you can pick and choose which way you want to make it and for what occasion.

The GF/CF frosting I use is Betty Crocker® white frosting. Although it has more additives than I usually like to use, such as corn syrup and modified corn starch, for the occasional special cake, I see no harm in using it. If you are creative, you can use food coloring and a cake decorator to make fancy shapes and designs and make a one of a kind cake for your child.

If, however, you want to try your hand at baking your own cakes, try my yellow cake recipe.

DONUTS AND CUPCAKES

Again, using a pre-packaged cake mix, you can make donuts, large or small, simply by purchasing special donut baking pans available in your local kitchen stores. It's a fun way to add a little variety to your child's desserts, and they can be easily frozen in individual baggies.

BROWNIES

There are some really great box mixes that make terrific GF/CF brownies. Peruse your local store and find the one that your child loves best. If you do not have time to bake, look for readymade brownies in the GF/CF aisle.

YELLOW CAKE

2 cups GF Flour Mix

2 tsp. Xantham Gum

1 1/2 cups sugar

1/2 cup CF margarine

1 cup prepared DariFree® Milk, Rice Milk or Soy Milk

3 1/2 tsp. of GF baking powder 1 tsp salt

1 tsp. GF Vanilla

3 eggs, slightly beaten

Heat oven to 350 °F. Grease and flour with GF/CF margarine and flour, a 13x9x2 pan or 2 round pans for a layer cake.

Sift flour, xantham gum, baking powder and salt in separate bowl.

Cream together margarine and sugar.

Add eggs and vanilla.

Alternate dry ingredients and dairy free milk.

Beat on high 3 minutes.

Pour into pan and bake 40-45 minutes or until toothpick inserted into middle of cake comes out clean. Cool and frost.

ASIAN PEAR FROSTING

This is a fun, whipped topping type of frosting that is easy to make.

    1 egg white
    1 cup sugar
    1 Asian pear- medium, peeled and grated

Put egg white into mixer and beat at high speed until egg starts to peak.
Add sugar and continue beating – continuing to form small peaks.
Add grated pear slowly and continue to beat mixture until it had a
whipped cream type texture. When it holds its peaks, you can frost your
cooled cake.

PUMPKIN CAKE

Grease a Bundt pan, and preheat oven to 350 °F

    2 2/3 cups sugar
    2/3 cup canola oil
    2/3 cup water
    4 eggs (beaten)
    2 tsp. vanilla
    1 can prepared pumpkin (16 oz.)
    3 ½ cup of GF Flour
    4 tsp. Xantham Gum
    1 ½ tsp. salt
    1 tsp ground cinnamon
    ½ tsp GF baking powder

Mix together sugar, canola oil, water, eggs and vanilla in mix master and beat on low until blended well.
Fold in pumpkin until smooth.
Sift together flour, xantham gum, salt, cinnamon and baking powder.
Add to wet ingredients.

Mix on low until smooth – about 4 minutes.
Pour into Bundt pan and bake for 1 hour until toothpick comes out clean.

Sprinkle with powdered sugar, if desired.

Note: This makes a large cake – cut into slices and freeze, then thaw for 1 minute in microwave and enjoy warm.

RED VELVET CAKE

Grease a two round pans, and preheat oven to 350°F

2 ½ cup of GF Flour
2 ½ tsp. Xantham Gum
1 ½ tsp. salt
½ tsp GF baking powder
1 tsp. Cocoa powder
1 ½ cups of sugar

1 ½ cups canola oil
1 cup soy buttermilk**
2 eggs lightly beaten
1 bottle of red food coloring (1 oz.)
1 tsp. white vinegar
1 tsp. GF vanilla extract

**Take 1 cup of soy milk (unflavored) and add two TBLS. of Lemon Juice. Let sit until thick.

Sift together dry ingredients in separate bowl.
Mix together oil, soy buttermilk, eggs, food coloring, white vinegar and vanilla extract.
Add sugar, beat at medium for about 1 minute.
Slowly add flour, baking soda, xantham gum, salt and cocoa powder at low speed until blended well.

Beat on high for 2 minutes.

Evenly pour into cake pans and bake at 350 °F for 30 minutes, or until toothpick comes out clean. Cool and frost. You can also make cupcakes – yields about 12 cupcakes.

Frost with Canned Frosting that is GF/CF or with Vanilla Frosting on next page.

VANILLA FROSTING:

    1/3 cup soy margarine
    3 cups powder sugar
    2 tsp of GF vanilla
    2-3 TBLS. Of play soy milk

Beat margarine until fluffy, adding sugar a little at a time.
Add vanilla
Add 1 TBLS. Of soy milk and beat until creamy.
Add another TBLS. Of soy milk to keep fluffy but spreadable.
Add more soy milk if needed.

Frost first layer, put on second layer, and then frost the top. Cover tightly to keep fresh.

BREADS AND ROLLS

For those of you who want a challenge, baking your own bread can be a true accomplishment.

To follow is a recipe that, although time consuming, makes the best home-made bread or dinner rolls.

> 3 cups of GF flour mix
> 3 tsp. Xantham Gum
> 1/4 cup sugar
> 1/2 cup Vance's DariFree® powder
> 1 tsp. unflavored gelatin
> 3/4 tsp. Salt
> 1 tsp. honey
> 1 pkg. of dry active yeast
> 1/2 cup lukewarm water
> 1/4 cup CF margarine
> 1 1/4 cup water
> 1 tsp. rice vinegar
> 1 egg plus 1/3 cup + 1 Tbsp. of liquid egg whites, beat together

Grease two loaf pans.

Sift flour, xantham gum and salt. Add milk powder, gelatin, and sugar. Blend well with regular beater.

Dissolve 2 tsp of sugar in 1/2 cup lukewarm water and add yeast. Let sit. Put water in saucepan with margarine and heat until melted.

Turn mixer on low and blend dry ingredients.

Slowly add water, margarine and vinegar – blend well.

Add egg and egg whites.

Pour in yeast water and beat at highest speed for 4 minutes.

The dough is more cake like than bread like, but do not be concerned.

Spray bread pans or muffin pans with non-stick spray. Put dough into loaf pans and let rise until doubled (about 40 minutes). Bake in pre-heated 400°F oven for 40-50 minutes until brown and loaf sounds hollow when tapped.

For rolls, place in muffin tins and let rise until doubled. Bake for about 25 minutes.

For added flavor you can brush the loaves or rolls with melted CF margarine.

Cut loaves with electric knife before freezing.

PIZZA CRUST

1 pkg. active dry yeast
1 cup warm water (105° to 115°)
2 1/2 cups GF flour
2 tablespoons of canola oil
1 tsp. sugar
1 tsp. salt

Dissolve yeast in warm water. Stir together remaining ingredients. Add yeast; mix vigorously – about 20 strokes. Let rest 5 minutes. Roll out to 2 personal size pizza crusts or one large pizza.

Top with sauce and other toppings, bake in oven 400 ° F oven 15-20 minutes.

INGREDIENTS TO AVOID

There are so many different types of additives to our foods these days, and it is mind boggling to keep up with them all. How many foods did you eat just today, that you really did not know what you were ingesting?

That morning cereal, you probably had niacin amide, or tricalcium phosphate. Do we really know what they are or what they do? Probably not. Thank goodness the box says "CONTAINS WHEAT AND SOY INGREDIENTS." I do not have to look any farther.

That said, I want to try and give you the quick buzz words so that you know what to look for when purchasing foods. I have even taught my daughter to look for these so that she knows if she can have particular foods.

WHEAT

> All Purpose Flour
> Barley
> Graham
> Oat
> Rye
> Semolina
> Modified Food Starch (unless it says specifically corn, it
> is derived from wheat flour)
> Malt
> Spelt

DAIRY

Lactose
Magnesium Caseinate
Caseinate
Milk Fat
Milk Solids
Buttermilk Solids
Whey Other Suspect Ingredients

Caramel color may also be suspect–watch your child's reaction if they had something with caramel coloring.

Mono and diglycerides – these may contain wheat, but can also be derived from corn. You may need to check with the manufacturer.

MSG is safe as far as GF/CF, but not recommended.

RECOMMENDED READING

Just as your child is unique, so are the books you may choose to read. Reading is my thing. I can take a book, devour it quickly and pick out information I think might work with my child. Even today and I try and devise study guides and tools to help my daughter study and cope with the "normal" world around her.

Below are just a few of my favorites which give help and insight to starting the diet plus other non-traditional ways you may want to help your child. Just go online and search "Autism" and an array of resources are at your fingertips. Choose wisely, do not overwhelm yourself. Be like a sifter – sort through the information, keep what appeals to you and discard the rest. You can always go back and pick up the information and start again.

The Child with Special Needs: Encouraging Intellectual Emotional Growth, Stanley Greenspan, Serena Wieder, Robin Simons, DaCapo Press, 1998.

Facing Autism: Giving Parents Reasons for Hope and Guidance for Help, Lynn M. Hamilton, Waterbrook Press, 2000.

Ten Things Every Child with Autism Wishes You Knew, Ellen Natbohn, Future Horizons, 2005.

The Care & Keeping of You – American Girl Series of books that focuses on young girls and growing up and questions about their changing bodies.

The Social Skills Picture Book, Jed Baker, Ph.D. Future Horizons, 2001

Thinking in Pictures and other reports from my Life with Autism, Temple Grandin, First Vintage Books, 1995.

Unraveling the Mysteries of Autism and Pervasive Development Disorder, Karyn Seroussi, Simon and Schuster, 2000.

A SPECIAL NOTE OF THANKS.....

My journey began 17 years ago, but my daughter's progress has been amazing and I could not have done it without the following people!

Dr. Christine Decker, Psychologist, PsyD, LCPC, Long Grove Psychological Associates.

Dr. Pat Purcell, East Louisville Pediatrics – she diagnosed Vicky at 2 ½.

First Steps (KY) – for pointing me in the right direction.

Jefferson County School System, Louisville, KY – their quick response to testing and placing her.

Lyndon Pre-school – to all the specialists and teacher who helped Vicky cope in a school setting with other children.

Kentuckiana Children's Center – for their guidance in the diet, and their support in finding alternative ideas to helping her.

Easter Seals of Louisville – For their outstanding help and efforts in speech and occupational therapy.

Dr. John Hicks – a DAN! Doctor who helped Vicky rid her system of contaminants and balance her immune system.

Back in the Saddle – Hippo Therapy and "Tweety" the horse – for giving Vicky confidence.

School Districts 46 and 127 – Grayslake, IL – for their continuing efforts with her IEP and their outstanding special education department.

University of Dubuque – Dubuque, IA – for giving Vicky a chance at college.

My family and friends who have put with the tantrums, food difficulties, altering their plans last minute and just plain supporting our family.

A very special thank you to my husband, Eugene Kulig, for always being willing to put up with any ideas I had (or still have). I remember when Vicky was going to Hippotherapy (therapy on horseback) and insurance decided they did not want to pay for it any more, he let me buy a horse! Without his love and support, Vicky would not be where she is today!

REFERENCES

Kulig, Natalie A. *The Simple Way to Start the Gf/CF Diet: An Easy Guide to Implementing the Gluten Free/casein Free Diet for Your Child with Autism*. U.S.: Trafford Pub, 2009. Print.

My Chemical Romance, "Welcome to the Black Parade" Lyrics, The Black Parade, 2006

Perle Kingsley, Emily. "Welcome to Holland." *Welcome to Holland*. Our-Kids, n.d. Web. 04 Oct. 2016. <http://www.our-kids.org/Archives/Holland.html>.

Sinclair, Jim. "DO NOT MOURN FOR US." *Don't Mourn For Us*. Autism Network, n.d. Web. 04 Oct. 2016. <http://www.autreat.com/dont_mourn.html>.

Made in the USA
Lexington, KY
16 November 2017